## THE
# CONTAINER GARDEN
*month-by-month*

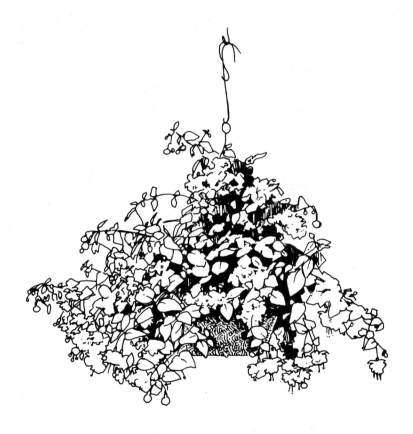

# THE
# CONTAINER GARDEN

*month-by-month*

## JACKIE BENNETT

**David & Charles**

*Photographs by Clive Nichols*

**A DAVID & CHARLES BOOK**

Copyright © Jackie Bennett

First published 1994

Jackie Bennett has asserted her right to be identified as author
of this work in accordance with the Copyright, Designs and
Patents Act 1988.

A catalogue record for this book is available from the British
Library.

ISBN 0 7153 0153 5

Illustrations by Maggie Raynor
Book design by Di Knapp

Typeset by ABM Typographics Ltd, Hull
and printed in Italy
by New Interlitho SpA
for David & Charles
Brunel House   Newton Abbot   Devon

# CONTENTS

Introduction   7

## JANUARY   10
*Practical project: Planning a balcony garden*   16

## FEBRUARY   18
*Practical project: Making an alpine trough garden*   24

## MARCH   28
*Practical project: Planting ferns in containers*   34

## APRIL   40
*Practical project: Making a miniature water garden*   46

## MAY   48
*Practical project: Planting and fixing a hanging basket*   54

## JUNE   58
*Practical project 1: Planting and fixing a windowbox*   64
*Practical project 2: Controlling container garden pests*   68

## JULY   70
*Practical project: Planting a herb/strawberry pot*   76

## AUGUST   80
*Practical project: Planting and fixing wall pots*   86

## SEPTEMBER   90
*Practical project: Planting up a chimney pot*   96

## OCTOBER   100
*Practical project: Planning and planting a winter display*   106

## NOVEMBER   110
*Practical project: Growing lilies in pots*   116

## DECEMBER   118
*Practical project: Growing roses in containers*   124

Appendix 1: *Growing Fruit and Vegetables in Containers*   128

Appendix 2: *Recommended Plants for Container Growing*   134

Appendix 3: *Unusual Ideas for Plant Containers*   139

Useful Addresses   140     Acknowledgements   142

Further Reading   142     Index   143

# INTRODUCTION

 As pressure on land resources continues to grow and buildings take priority over open spaces, an ever-increasing number of people do not, and never will have, access to a fully fledged garden. What we often do have, of course, are window ledges and front steps, balconies and basements, rooftops and backyards. What we lose in grass and borders we can gain by meeting a new challenge: to become gardeners without gardens.

Far from being the poor relation of conventional horticulture, growing plants in containers is one of the most rewarding – and creative – ways to garden. Even those who do have a garden often also have a paved area, patio or terrace on which to place pots and tubs of plants, and together this new wave of container gardeners is taking the horticultural world by storm. Commercial growers are being persuaded to produce sensibly compact plants and easy-to-handle composts, while garden centres try to encourage us with 'patio collections', self-watering planters and stylish pottery. Every style of gardening that can be expressed in a full-sized garden can be replicated in the container garden, be it a romantic, flower-filled courtyard, a balcony crammed with edible produce or a low-maintenance windowbox.

One of the beauties of container gardening is that it can be adapted to suit all tastes and pockets. It is possible to buy large, mature plants ready-planted in pots to create an instant effect – at a price. But for most of us, it is more realistic to build up a collection of pots and permanent plants gradually, creating a few splashes of instant colour with seasonal annuals.

*Pots of lilies, pelargoniums and nicotiana make an impressive display in a city courtyard*

A container garden is mobile, adaptable and eminently suited to changing lifestyles. Young people rarely, if ever, have a permanent fixed abode, so pots can travel with them. Adults, too, are realising the good sense of bringing the garden nearer to hand: why walk halfway down the garden to enjoy the fragrance of summer lilies or to collect a few herbs and tomatoes for the evening meal, when you can have them on your doorstep?

Perhaps the best thing of all about a contained garden is that it gives you control: over weeds, over the size of the plants, and over colour combinations – a definite advantage if you're just starting out in gardening, or if you simply want to be less of a slave to the garden hoe and pruning shears.

## BACK TO BASICS

With a few exceptions, it is possible to grow just about anything in a pot which can be grown in a bed – fruit, vegetables, herbs, roses, bulbs, annual and perennial flowers, climbers, shrubs and trees. As with any garden, the main considerations are the growing medium (in this case, potting compost) and the amount of sun, shade and shelter the plants will receive.

The advent of container-grown plants (those raised entirely in containers) means that planting can, in theory, be carried out at any time. In practice, however, it is never a good idea to plant in cold, wet or frosty weather; nor is it sensible to plant during a hot spell in summer, when the plants will have to work extra hard to adjust to their new environment. (If you do buy plants in the summer, leave them in a shady corner for a day or two after repotting, and only gradually introduce them to full sun.) Container gardeners tend to neglect autumn as a planting time, putting all their efforts into

### KEY TO PLANT LISTS

Throughout the book you will find lists of plants for specific purposes. These have been coded as follows:

| | |
|---|---|
| **A** | **Hardy annual** |
| **HHA** | **Half-hardy annual** |
| **B** | **Biennial** |
| **P** | **Perennial** |
| **E** | **Evergreen** |
| **D** | **Deciduous** |

### PLANT TYPES

Plants are described by their commonly used names (where applicable) as well as by their botanical name. Plants should be considered hardy unless stated otherwise.

#### ANNUAL
Germinates and flowers the same year, then dies.

#### BIENNIAL
Germinates one year, flowers the next, then dies.

#### PERENNIAL
Survives for many years.

#### BULB
Underground storage organ, developed from bases of the leaves.

#### CORM
Underground storage organ, developed from the bases of the stems.

#### RHIZOME
Underground stem.

#### TUBER
Underground organ, developed from the roots and underground stems.

#### SHRUB
Woody plant, branching from ground level, usually smaller than a tree.

#### TREE
Woody plant with a central trunk, usually taller growing than a shrub.

spring and summer, but the cooler weather and rains of autumn are very beneficial to newly potted plants, giving the roots a good chance to get established before the hard weather arrives. This is also a good time to plant up hanging baskets and pots for winter interest and colour.

If there could be just two golden rules of container gardening, mine would be: first, buy the largest containers you can afford. The most common mistake is to use pots that are too small, so that the plants grow bare, leggy and starved. To the plant, the container is its whole world. It must provide water, air and nutrients, and give the roots room to develop. This doesn't mean that small plants should be put in huge pots – but it does mean that you need a good range of pot sizes, so that plants can be potted on regularly. Second, buy more compost than you think you will possibly need. Plants in containers should never be put in garden soil, which may be devoid of nutrients and full of pests. Potting compost is sterile, pleasant to use and contains everything your plants need for their first few months of life.

### HOW TO USE THE BOOK

The aim of this book is to make the information which you, the gardener, need accessible at any time of year. So, whether you pick it up in the depths of winter or at the height of summer, you will be able to find out immediately what tasks need doing that month, what's in flower and how to deal with any special problems the weather conditions might bring.

Each chapter is divided into four sections: an introduction, a checklist of the main tasks and instructions on how to carry them out, profiles of plants which are at their best, and a practical project for those who want to increase their range of planting ideas and skills.

Obviously, for each month only a limited number of plants can be featured. I have endeavoured to include a good cross-section of trees and shrubs, flowering plants and evergreens, bulbs and bedding plants – Appendix II gives a fuller list of suitable plants. But even this selection should not be taken as written in indelible ink. Plants are notoriously temperamental: some will not thrive, even though you give them all the textbook care and attention; many more will surprise you by their tenacity in less-than-ideal conditions. Learn to recognise the plants that do well in your particular mini-climate, and then try out a few new ones. The only restrictions are space, and your own imagination.

### SEASONS AND MONTHS

It is difficult to be precise about which month a particular flower will bloom or when, for example, spring will start. This will vary from area to area and the differences can be even more pronounced in a container garden, which has its own particular microclimate. There can even be differences between an exposed roof terrace and a sheltered, south-facing patio belonging to the same house. However, under average conditions, the seasons used throughout the book correspond to the following months:

**SPRING**
Early: March
Mid: April
Late: May

**SUMMER**
Early: June
Mid: July
Late: August

**AUTUMN**
Early: September
Mid: October
Late: November

**WINTER**
Early: December
Mid: January
Late: February

# JANUARY

This time of year almost certainly brings chill winds and possibly a flurry of snow. The truth is, most self-respecting gardeners are tucked up indoors, only venturing down the garden path to tie in the odd wind-blown climber or perhaps bravely to plant a shrub received as a seasonal gift.

But this month is also the traditional time for new beginnings, and a container garden, whether it consists of a single windowbox or an extensive patio, will probably benefit from a rethink. The containers themselves are arguably the most important component and may well be the most expensive: use this month to consider what could be added to your collection.

Far less costly are the seed catalogues, out in abundance now. There's a good reason for making your seed choice early – and not only because the catalogues make such good, escapist fireside reading. Winter can lull gardeners into a false sense of security, and the early spring sowing times seem to come and go faster than the speed of light. Don't miss the chance to raise nasturtiums, marigolds and sweet peas from seed – summer will be the poorer without them.

If your containers are already in good shape, you should be enjoying the permanent foliage of ivies, box and bay, with yuccas and conifers like Chamaecyparis lawsoniana 'Ellwoods Pillar' adding bold, architectural outlines. These plants are undaunted by frost and snow and, in fact, a layer of either actually enhances their shape and gives them an even sharper visual dimension. For colour, make a note to plant up some winter pansies for next year.

If all else fails, the ubiquitous snowdrop will brighten the gloomiest winter day.

# tasks

## FOR THE

# *month*

### SEEDS TO ORDER

**Ageratum** HHA
**Alyssum** A
*Campanula carpatica* P
**Foxglove** *(Digitalis)* B
**French marigold** *(Tagetes patula)*
HHA
*Mesembryanthemum criniflorium*
HHA
**Nasturtium** A
**Pansy** *(Viola* × *wittrockiana)* A
*Phlox drummondii* HHA
**Pot marigold** *(Calendula)* A
**Snapdragon** *(Antirrhinum)* HHA
**Sweet pea** *(Lathyrus odoratus)* A
**Sweet William** *(Dianthus
barbatus)* B
**Tobacco plant** *(Nicotiana)* HHA
**Tomatoes and salad crops**
**(see p132 for varieties)**

*DRIP TRAYS*

*Don't forget to buy plant saucers
or drip trays for every pot you
will be using. These prevent
excess water draining away
when the plant is watered from
the top and will also collect
rainwater, which is then available
for the plant to draw up as
needed.*

*For more container ideas see
p139.*

## CHECKLIST

☐ Order seeds and plantlets
☐ Choose containers
☐ Plant fruit trees, shrubs and roses (reminder)

### ORDERING SEEDS AND PLANTLETS

Ordering through seed catalogues is the easiest and most efficient way to buy seeds for spring sowing. More and more nurseries are gearing their catalogues to the container gardener and including special collections for patio tubs, windowboxes and hanging baskets. A relatively new development is the range of seedlings, rooted cuttings and 'plug plants' now on offer, all of which save you the bother of actually sowing the seed yourself. Seeds you order now will be dispatched straight away, although seedlings and plantlets will probably not be sent out until early or mid-spring (see Useful Addresses, p140).

### CHOOSING CONTAINERS

Midwinter is a good time to take stock of your pots, tubs, windowboxes and hanging baskets to see if they meet your needs. A contained garden can be expensive to plan from scratch, so start early and spread the cost over several months. At the end of the day, the choice of containers is a matter of personal taste, but there are various factors that need to be taken into consideration.

First, consider the building materials of the house, walls and paved areas. Bright colours and geometric shapes can look incongruous against mellow stone; likewise, ornately decorated urns look out of place against clean-cut, modern architectural lines. Second, think about the style of garden you want to achieve – Mediterranean, cottage, oriental, formal – each will need a rather different combination of containers.

Finally, but by no means as an afterthought, consider the plants themselves. Each plant has an ideal container size and shape, and putting the two together is something that starts with trial and error but becomes second nature with experience. As a starting point, the minimum depth of soil for even the smallest plant (except alpines, which thrive on shallow soil) is 20cm (8in) and your collection of pots should range upwards from this. Remember that

plants will move up through the pot sizes as they develop from year to year. Once plants are at their full size, give them the most generous-sized pots you can afford. The more compost a container can hold, the more water and nutrients are available to the plant. Too small a pot will result in plants that dry out quickly and are starved of the food they need.

### Materials

■ *Terracotta*
Probably the most popular container material and rightly so, terracotta is relatively inexpensive, blends in well with most settings and is good for plants. The porous clay allows water to evaporate naturally, preventing waterlogging of the roots, and offers reasonable insulation against extremes of temperature. However, in areas prone to frost the water absorbed by the pot can freeze, causing the clay to contract and possibly crack the pot. To avoid this problem, choose frost-proof terracotta that has been fired to a very high temperature.

■ *Plastic*
Almost as popular as terracotta because of its low cost and light weight. Plastic makes durable, convenient plant containers, particularly for growing large quantities of seedlings or annual flowers.

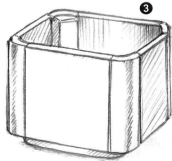

Plastic is very useful on balconies and roof gardens, where a heavier material might be a problem. Plastic containers need to be monitored for waterlogging, but do offer roots adequate protection against heat and cold. Plastic becomes brittle after some years of use.

### ■ *Wood*

Wooden Versailles tubs, half-barrels, troughs and windowboxes are widely available, usually pre-treated with a non-toxic wood preservative. They are more expensive than plastic, but the price compares favourably with terracotta. The beauty of wooden containers is their large capacity, particularly in the case of half-barrels which can happily accommodate trees, shrubs and climbers. Wood is a good insulator and waterlogging is not a problem. Rot-resistant hardwoods are the best choice, but any treated wood will last many years if regularly maintained.

### ■ *Stone*

Natural stone containers are too expensive for most people, although they are undoubtedly beautiful in the right setting. Stone is very heavy and therefore best used in a position where it can remain permanently and where it will become increasingly weathered with age. Stone urns or troughs need no maintenance and will probably outlast the plants themselves. A less costly alternative is to buy pots made from reconstituted stone, which is powdered stone in a cement base. Reconstituted stone containers are widely available and, although still heavy, are easier to move around the garden than real stone.

### ■ *Ceramics*

Ceramic pots are more often used indoors, where they are less likely to get chipped and broken. However, large Chinese glazed pots are extremely decorative and relatively sturdy, and are particularly effective for displaying oriental plants such as bamboos and acers. The glazed finish means that the clay is not porous, so they need careful watering to avoid waterlogging. The water never seeps through so the patterning remains intact, and with care these pots will stay looking good for many years. As with terracotta, check that the clay has been fired to a high enough temperature to resist frost.

### ■ *Glass-reinforced plastic (Glassfibre)*

This is now increasingly used to imitate other materials such as antique lead in caskets and windowboxes. It is strong, lightweight and frostproof, but not always cheap. Ornately decorated containers can be as expensive as the same piece made in clay or stone and, in fact, as the material improves it is becoming harder to tell the difference without feeling the texture and the weight.

## PLANTS TO BUY AS SEEDLINGS, PLUGS OR ROOTED CUTTINGS

**Ivy leaf and zonal pelargonium**
**Impatiens**
**Begonia**
**Fuchsia**
**Pansy**
**Petunia**
**Lobelia**
**Helichrysum**
**Nepeta**

## SHORT TERM POTS

*Recycled cellulose fibre is a short-life material which nevertheless has its uses in the container garden. The knobbly brown appearance is by no means attractive, but this can be disguised with trailing plants and by grouping pots together. Fibre pots really come into their own when a large number of containers is needed for a short display – for example, for spring bulbs or summer annuals. The containers can then be discarded in the autumn when the flowers are finished. Bulbs grown for one season can be put straight into the garden still in their pots, where the fibre will gradually biodegrade.*

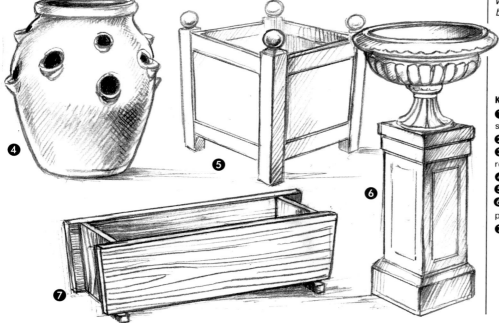

## KEY

❶ Terracotta pot with matching saucer
❷ Terracotta wall pot
❸ Plastic pot with built-in water reservoir
❹ Terracotta strawberry pot
❺ Wooden Versailles tub
❻ Reconstituted stone urn and pedestal
❼ Wooden trough

# plants
## OF THE
## *month*

## IRIS
### *(Iris histrioides* 'Major')

One of the first of the bulbous irises to flower, this pretty little plant often appears in early winter and survives all weathers, including snow. Its compact height makes it a good choice for pots and windowboxes, although the leaves do grow over 30cm (12in) high in the spring.

| | |
|---|---|
| type | Bulb |
| flowers | Bright blue; in winter, before the leaves are fully grown |
| height | 10cm (4in) |
| spread | 5-10cm (2-4in) |
| planting | Autumn, 5-7.5cm (2-3in) deep in groups of five or more, 10cm (4in) apart |
| site | Open, sunny position |
| compost | Well-drained, multi-purpose or alpine mix (see p20) |
| care | Water regularly, but ensure the compost never becomes waterlogged. After flowering, apply a liquid feed once a month for three months to build up the bulbs for the following year |
| propagation | Divide bulbs after the foliage has died down. Replant bulbs and offsets immediately |
| related species | *Iris reticulata* flowers a little later than *I.histrioides*, but is equally suitable for windowboxes (see p66) |

## WINTER-FLOWERING VIBURNUM
### *(Viburnum tinus)*

A useful shrub for the container garden, *V. tinus* is smaller than the more widely-grown *Viburnum bodnantense*, although it will eventually reach a size that will require a large barrel or patio tub. The pink or white flowers appear from late autumn right through until the end of spring, while the evergreen foliage means that it never looks bare.

| | |
|---|---|
| type | Evergreen shrub |
| flowers | White with pink buds; late autumn to late spring |
| height | To 2.2m (7ft) |
| spread | To 2.2m (7ft) |
| planting | Early to mid-autumn, or spring |
| site | Full sun; protected from cold winds |
| compost | Loam-based |
| care | Prune in late spring, thinning out any old or damaged wood |
| propagation | Take semi-ripe cuttings in late summer or early autumn |
| varieties | 'Eve Price' has pink flowers; 'Variegatum' has golden-variegated leaves |
| related species | *Viburnum davidii* is a compact, evergreen, summer-flowering species. The flowers are white and are often followed by turquoise-blue berries |

 ## LAWSON CYPRESS
### *(Chamaecyparis lawsoniana)*

A container garden should have one or two conifers to give shape and structure in winter and the dwarf forms of the lawson cypress are ideal for this purpose. Consider these conifers as a permanent part of the planting; they are slow-growing and generally do not like to be lifted. To relieve the darkness of the foliage, surround them with early-flowering bulbs such as crocus or miniature iris. Then, in summer, move the pots to the back of the display and let more showy flowers come to the fore.

| | |
|---|---|
| type | Evergreen conifer |
| height | Maximum: 3m (10ft); many forms are smaller |
| spread | Maximum: 1m (3ft) |
| planting | Mid-autumn or mid-spring; in tubs, troughs or pots |
| site | Sun or light shade; golden forms retain their colour better in full sun |
| compost | Well-drained, multi-purpose |
| care | Feeding not necessary during first year. In subsequent years, use a liquid feed monthly during spring and summer. Water well in hot, dry weather |
| propagation | From cuttings taken in early autumn |
| varieties | 'Ellwoodii' forms a grey-green columnar tree which will eventually reach 3m (10ft) – suitable for growing in a half-barrel; 'Ellwood's Pillar' grows no more than 75cm (2½ft high); 'Green Globe' is a miniature version with bright green foliage, reaching 30cm (12in) |
| related species | Dwarf forms of *Chamaecyparis pisifera* are also suited to container growing, particularly 'Nana', a dark green, low-growing bush to 45cm (18in). *Chamaecyparis obtusa* 'Nana Aurea' forms a compact mound of golden foliage, 60 × 60cm (2 × 2ft) |

| | |
|---|---|
| related species | *L. standishii* is similar but grows to a more compact 1.2m (4ft). *L. periclymenum* is the vigorous summer-flowering climbing honeysuckle; it can be grown in a large tub or barrel but will need regular pruning to keep it within bounds |

## COMMON SNOWDROP
### *(Galanthus nivalis)*

Generally grown naturalised in grass, the snowdrop is often neglected as a subject for growing in pots. Yet it needs very little care, and will flower and bring interest in the coldest of winters.

| | |
|---|---|
| type | Bulb |
| flowers | White with green markings on the inner petals; mid- to late winter |
| height | 15cm (6in) |
| spread | 15cm (6in) |
| planting | 10cm (4in) deep, 15cm (6in) apart in early autumn, or in late winter whilst still in flower |
| site | Sun or partial shade |
| compost | Loam-based |
| care | Keep well watered during the growing season; do not allow the compost to dry out |
| propagation | Divide the bulbs while still in flower and replant immediately |
| varieties | 'Flora-plena' has double flowers; 'S. Arnott' is taller than the species; 'Viridapicis' has green markings on the outer as well as the inner petals |

## WINTER HONEYSUCKLE
### *(Lonicera fragrantissima)*

A wonderful wall shrub for winter interest and cover. In mild areas the leaves are retained all year round, and from early winter onwards the creamy-white flowers give off a strong perfume. Good for planting against a wall near the entrance door, where the scent will be appreciated as visitors brush past it.

| | |
|---|---|
| type | Semi-evergreen shrub |
| flowers | Creamy-white, fragrant; early winter to early spring |
| height | 2m (6ft) |
| spread | 2m (6ft) |
| planting | Mid-to late spring against a wall, fence or trellis |
| site | Sun or partial shade – ideally with the roots in shade and the foliage in sun. A basement, where the stems can reach up into the light, would be suitable |
| compost | Well-drained, multi-purpose |
| care | Benefits from a mulch of well-rotted compost or manure in spring. Water well and liquid feed monthly during the spring and summer. No regular pruning needed – take out old wood after flowering to keep it looking tidy |
| propagation | By hardwood cuttings in early to mid-autumn |

# *practical* project

## PLANNING A BALCONY GARDEN

At first sight a balcony may seem to offer a somewhat restricted space for gardening, but it does provide a great deal of scope for planting in containers. Plants on a balcony are primarily intended to be viewed from the inside, whether it adjoins a living room, bedroom or kitchen. In fact, the siting of the balcony might dictate the kind of plants you grow there: fragrant species outside the bedroom, for example, or herbs and salad vegetables near the kitchen. Although there are some unavoidable problems with balcony gardening, they can be overcome with sensible planning.

### SAFETY FIRST

■ *Always check the structural condition of your balcony. Look for signs of cracking, particularly where it joins the main wall. If in doubt, get expert advice.*

■ *Ensure that the boundary railings are in good order. Any balcony which will be used as an outdoor room should have sturdy boundaries to prevent falls.* ■

### STRUCTURE AND WEIGHT

The first consideration in planning your balcony garden must be the strength of the balcony and whether it can support the additional weight of pots, compost and plants. One answer is to use lightweight plastic, fibreglass or cellulose containers and a soilless, peat (or peat substitute) compost. Bear in mind that soilless composts are difficult to re-wet once they have dried out and will need to be checked and watered more regularly than loam-based types.

Wooden windowboxes or troughs are not unduly heavy, but it is best to avoid large wooden half-barrels. Small pots can be terracotta or ceramic – in fact, this is preferable if they are not to blow over in the wind. Remember that the weakest part of a balcony is the centre, so keep pots and troughs to the outside edges.

### SCREENING

Strong winds and air frosts can play havoc with plants, so they will need to be screened – without spoiling the view. Many balconies already have railings, which are ideal, particularly if climbing plants are encouraged to twine around them. If you need to erect a screen, welded iron railings are the safest option.

They break the wind but allow enough air through to prevent the turbulent currents associated with solid walls or fences.

### BALCONY SURFACE

If the balcony has a tar-based finish which melts and becomes sticky in the sun, one solution is to overlay it with wooden decking. This is usually bought in sections, which makes it easy to lay and to take up. The wood will not add undue weight and the decking will help to spread the load of the containers.

### PLANTING

One of the main considerations for balcony gardeners is what to do with plants that have finished flowering or those that need to be brought inside over winter, particularly if space is limited indoors as well as out. Although gardeners do overwinter pelargoniums and fuchsias, it is probably better to discard them as they are not expensive to buy as small plants again in the spring. Likewise, buy cheap strips of bedding plants rather than raise annuals from seed; the effect is instant and there will be far less mess. For a permanent planting scheme which can stay in position all year round, choose a background of permanent shrubs, a few climbers such as ivy or *Hydrangea petiolaris*, a selection or herbs like rosemary, bay, thyme or mint, and then ring the changes with boxes of spring bulbs which can be lifted easily to give way to colourful summer bedding.

### NOTE
### Shady Problem

■ *Some balconies are cursed with overhanging masonry that stops rainfall reaching the plants and blocks out most of the sun. Don't give up on the idea of growing plants altogether, but consider using self-watering planters which have a reservoir of moisture ready for the plant to draw up as needed. There are also lots of shade-loving foliage plants like hostas, hellebores and ivies which can provide a dark backdrop to more showy, shade-tolerant flowering climbers such as* Clematis montana *or* C. 'Hagley Hybrid' ■

*TWO PLANS FOR A RECTANGULAR BALCONY*

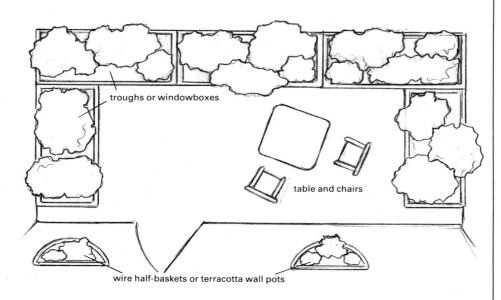

troughs or windowboxes

table and chairs

wire half-baskets or terracotta wall pots

*This balcony is treated like a large windowsill, with troughs or windowboxes along the edges planted with trailing and low-growing plants. The result is a simple, neat-looking balcony, leaving room for dining out.*

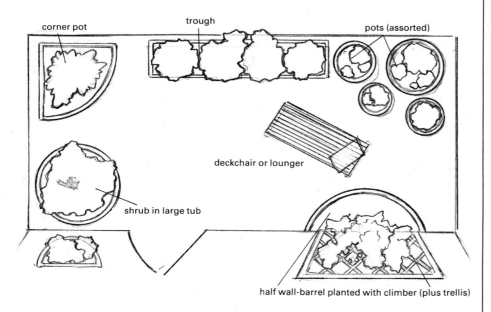

corner pot

trough

pots (assorted)

deckchair or lounger

shrub in large tub

half wall-barrel planted with climber (plus trellis)

*A more informal effect is achieved by grouping pots together and planting a mixture of shrubs, trailing plants and climbers. Even with the extra planting, there is still room for a sun lounger.*

## WHAT TO GROW

### CLIMBERS
**Clematis (*Clematis* × 'Jackmanii', *C. montana, C.* × 'Hagley Hybrid')
Climbing hydrangea (*Hydrangea petiolaris*)
Ivy (*Hedera helix*)
Passion flower (*Passiflora caerulea*)
Summer jasmine (*Jasminum officinale*) (scented)**

### VEGETABLES
**Choose shallow-rooted salad crops such as tomatoes, radishes and spring onions to grow in pots, or plant peas and beans in windowboxes and train them up trellis for an instant windbreak.**

### ANNUALS
**Choose species that will not mind the drying wind:
Lobelia • Nasturtium • Pelargonium (tender perennial) • Petunia • Salvia**

### SHRUBS
**Choose low-growing varieties that can stand drying out by the wind and sun:
Hebe (*Hebe pinguifolia* 'Pagei')
Heather (*Erica carnea*)
Lavender (*Lavandula angustifolia*)
*Potentilla fruticosa*
Mexican orange (*Choisya ternata*)**

### HERBS
**Most kitchen herbs are suitable for balcony growing. Choose from:
Bay • Chervil • Chives • Marjoram • Mint • Parsley • Rosemary • Sage • Thyme**

# FEBRUARY

This is often the least inviting time of the year for gardeners, with a good chance of cold, wet weather and the ever-present danger of frost and snow. Despite the gloomy outlook, the container garden should not be neglected. There are plenty of tasks to be carried out in the run-up to spring and any unseasonally mild days should be utilised to the full.

This is the month during which last autumn's forethought starts to pay dividends. Pots crammed with cheerful crocus, Iris reticulata *and early daffodils are the perfect antidote to a winter's day. Evergreens also come into their own, wonderfully resilient against biting winds and rain, although blustery weather can be a problem for container plants at this time of year. Make sure that pots are heavy enough not to topple over in a gale and pay particular attention to those on steps, balconies and roof gardens. Large pots and barrels will not be affected but smaller, lightweight containers should be grouped together and weighted down with planks of wood or bricks. Ensure that climbers are tied in securely to their supports.*

Apart from bulbs, it is the shrubs grown in containers that provide interest and variety this month. The corkscrew hazel (Corylus avellana 'Contorta') *bears silky catkins just like its full-size, straight-branched relative, as does the willow* Salix caprea 'Pendula'. *For colour,* Daphne mezereum *is in flower with its pink, fragrant sprays and, in some areas, camellias are beginning their show with a range of colours from white through pink to red and deep crimson, depending on variety. Early camellias can be damaged by wind, frost and rain, so if possible stand the pots in a porch. If left outside, avoid a position where the early morning sun after a night of frost can damage the blooms.*

# tasks

## FOR THE

## *month*

*'INVISIBLE' MENDING*
*Terracotta pots can be 'invisibly'*
*mended by adding a small amount*
*of powdered crock to the*
*adhesive. Grind a small piece of*
*broken pot in a mortar and pestle*
*and mix it into the glue on an old*
*lid or saucer; then apply sparingly*
*to the joints.*

## CHECKLIST

☐ Clean and repair containers
☐ Buy compost
☐ Lift and divide snowdrops
☐ Cut back overwintered pelargoniums and fuchsias
☐ Prune clematis
☐ Repot fruit trees

### CLEANING AND PREPARING POTS

Pots can now be assembled and cleaned in readiness for planting. Over time, used terracotta pots tend to become encrusted with mineral salts and this patina can be part of a pot's character. If a clean surface is preferred these deposits can be removed with a stiff brush or wire wool. Soaking pots first in a solution of water and ammonium sulphate helps to loosen the deposit.

### NOTE

■ *Clay is very porous and, when dry, absorbs a lot of water. Give new terracotta pots a good soak before planting them up to avoid water being absorbed by the pot rather than by the compost* ■

### Mending and refurbishing pots and containers

Broken clay pots can be glued together using an epoxy-resin adhesive. Make sure that the surfaces are clean and dry before starting. Pots that are broken into several pieces will need to be wired together once the joints have been glued. Wrap lengths of wire around the whole pot, pull taut and leave in place until the fixative is completely dry.

If untreated, new wooden containers should be painted with a non-toxic wood preservative – *not* creosote. Old containers which are showing signs of wear and tear can be treated at the same time.

New wooden half-barrels should have drainage holes drilled in the base before planting, and to prevent rusting the metal bands can be painted with an anti-rust paint.

### CHOOSING COMPOST

The most widely used composts are the **multi-purpose soilless** types, which are generally peat-based. They are suitable for a wide range of plants at all stages of growth, from seed sowing to maturity. They are also light, clean and relatively inexpensive, but do have a tendency to dry out rapidly, shrinking away from the pot sides, and can be difficult to re-water. They contain fertiliser which will feed plants for up to three months after potting;

thereafter, regular feeding is needed.

For alpine plants, which prefer a well-drained medium, mix one-third grit or gravel with two-thirds multi-purpose potting compost.

**Loam-based** composts contain loam with peat, sand or grit and a slow-release fertiliser. They come in different formulas according to the fertiliser content: low nutrient value for seedlings and cuttings; medium nutrient value for general purpose and small plants; high nutrient value for large plants and fast-growing crops like tomatoes. They are heavier and retain water better than peat-based composts, so make a good choice for trees, shrubs and climbers which are grown permanently in pots.

Acid-loving plants, such as rhododendrons and camellias, are often grown in special **lime-free ericaceous** composts, but will grow equally well in a peat-based or multi-purpose compost.

For gardeners who do not want to use peat there are various peat alternatives available, such as those based on **coir** fibre and timber by-products. As yet there is no conclusive evidence as to which give the best results, and it is worth experimenting with different kinds. These composts can be difficult to re-wet if allowed to dry out, so careful attention to watering is important, as is regular feeding.

**Growing bags** are particularly useful for food crops such as tomatoes, courgettes, peppers and strawberries. The compost contains a balanced selection of nutrients which will feed the plants until they are well established. As the bags are not particularly attractive, they are probably best concealed behind other pots.

### LIFTING AND DIVIDING SNOWDROPS

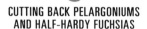

Snowdrops need to be moved while the leaves are still green and, since they must not be allowed to dry out, should be replanted immediately.

■ Lift crowded clumps as soon as the flowers fade, separate the bulbs carefully and replant at the same depth in smaller groups.

### CUTTING BACK PELARGONIUMS AND HALF-HARDY FUCHSIAS

Last year's pelargoniums and fuchsias which were brought indoors for the winter should be cut back now while they are still dormant.

■ Cut back all the fuchsia's side branches which produced flowers last year, leaving one or two buds on each. Cut back the pelargoniums to within 23cm (9in) of the base. Make the cuts just above a bud.

■ Remove the plants from their pots and tease the compost from around the roots, taking care not to damage them. Loose compost can be shaken away.

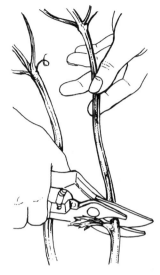

■ Repot into a pot just large enough to take the roots comfortably, using a loam-based cuttings compost. Water thoroughly. The plants will now start into growth again, ready to be put outside when the danger of frosts has passed.

### PRUNING CLEMATIS

Late-flowering clematis like *C* × 'Jackmanii,' *C.* 'Hagley Hybrid' and *C. viticella* should be cut back hard now, as they will flower on growth made this year. Cut all their

*Clematis after pruning*

stems back to just above the lowest pair of leaf buds.

### REPOTTING FRUIT TREES

Figs and other fruit trees that are in their second year of growth will need repotting. Lift the plant out carefully by its stem and remove as much soil as possible from the roots. Repot in a clean, same-size or slightly larger pot, using a loam-based compost (see opposite).

In subsequent years, the top 5cm (2in) of compost should be replaced with fresh.

*WATERING PELARGONIUMS AND FUCHSIAS*
*The best way to water plants that are very dry is to immerse the whole pot in a bucket of tepid water. Hold the pot under so that the water covers the soil surface, and anchor it down with a saucer to prevent the compost floating away. When the air bubbles have stopped, allow the pot to drain thoroughly before replacing it on the saucer.*

# plants
## OF THE
## *month*

### OREGON GRAPE
#### (*Mahonia aquifolium*)

This sturdy, evergreen shrub is worth growing for its eye-catching, glossy foliage and sprays of yellow flowers in late winter and early spring. It stays a more compact size than the widely grown garden hybrid *Mahonia × media* 'Charity', but the latter flowers earlier, often from late autumn. *M. aquifolium* has bunches of blue-black berries which appear after the flowers – hence its common name.

| | |
|---|---|
| type | Evergreen shrub |
| flowers | Fragrant, yellow; late winter to mid-spring |
| height | 1-1.5m (3-5ft) |
| spread | 1.5-2m (5-6ft) |
| planting | Early autumn or late spring |
| site | Sun or shade; tolerates wind and exposed positions, so useful for balconies and roof gardens |
| compost | Multi-purpose or loam-based |
| care | Keep the compost moist, particularly in periods of drought. No regular pruning needed |
| propagation | By softwood cuttings in summer |
| varieties | 'Atropurpurea' has red-purple leaves in winter |
| related species | *M. × media* 'Charity' grows to 3m (10ft) and has longer, deep yellow flowers from late autumn to late winter. |

*ALPINE CROCUS*
*Alpine crocus are ideal for growing in alpine troughs or in shallow terracotta 'pans'. For winter-flowering choose C. imperati with purple flowers, planted with the tiny yellow C. minimus, the smallest of all the spring-flowering species. Remember to use a well-drained compost – mix ordinary, multi-purpose potting compost with one-third grit or gravel. Top-dress the pots with gravel to increase surface drainage.*

## IRIS RETICULATA

*Iris reticulata* is particularly suitable for growing in pots, windowboxes and alpine troughs. The delicate blooms are scented and come into flower in late winter when there is little other colour in the garden.

| | |
|---|---|
| type | Bulb |
| flowers | Purple-blue with orange blaze, scented; late winter to early spring |
| height | 15cm (6in) |
| spread | 10cm (4in) |
| planting | Early autumn, in groups, 7.5cm (3in) deep, 10cm (4in) apart |
| site | Sunny; in pots, windowboxes, troughs |
| compost | Well-drained, multi-purpose or alpine mix (see p.20) |
| care | After flowering, feed once a month for three months with a liquid fertiliser to ensure healthy bulbs the following year |
| propagation | Divide the bulbs after the foliage has died down. Replant bulbs and offsets immediately |
| varieties | 'Cantab' has pale blue flowers; 'Harmony' is a royal blue; 'Pauline' is a purple-pink with white markings |

## DAPHNE
#### (*Daphne mezereum*)

This shrub lights up the patio in late winter with its upright stems of fragrant pink flowers. The branches are bare of leaves, making the flowers all the more noticeable. This daphne's compact habit makes it a good container subject. The flowers are followed by scarlet berries, giving the shrub a long season of interest.

| | |
|---|---|
| type | Deciduous shrub |
| flowers | Pink to purple; late winter to mid-spring |
| height | Up to 1.5m (5ft) |
| spread | 60cm-1.2m (2-4ft) |
| planting | Early autumn or spring |
| site | Sun or light shade |
| compost | Multi-purpose |
| care | No pruning required, but straggly growths can be removed in early spring |
| propagation | From semi-ripe cuttings in mid- or late summer |
| varieties | 'Alba' is a white variety with yellow fruits; 'Grandiflora' has |

larger purple flowers which start to appear in autumn

| related species | *Daphne cneorum* is a low-growing evergreen shrub which looks good in large stone troughs. The rose-pink flowers appear in late spring and early summer and are highly scented. Height: 15cm (6in); spread: 60cm (2ft) |

## CROCUS

Crocus are one of the mainstays of winter and early spring containers (there are also autumn species which are worth growing). The late-winter-flowering bulbs widely available from garden centres are usually from the parent species *Crocus chrysanthus* and numerous hybrid forms are now available. They are easy to grow and make ideal subjects for pots and windowboxes planted amongst other bulbs, combined with trailing ivies or planted beneath evergreen shrubs and conifers to give tubs a winter sparkle.

| type | Bulb |
| --- | --- |
| flowers | Yellow, purple, blue, cream and orange; late winter |
| height | 7.5cm (3in) |
| spread | 7.5cm (3in) |
| planting | Autumn, 5-7.5cm (2-3in) deep |
| site | Sunny; need protection from cold winds |
| compost | Well-drained, multi-purpose |
| care | Water well during spring and summer |

| propagation | As soon as the leaves turn brown, lift and separate any offsets and replant |
| --- | --- |
| varieties | 'E.A. Bowles' has rich yellow blooms; 'Snow Bunting' is white with an orange base |
| related species | The autumn-flowering *C. speciosus* is one of the easiest crocuses to grow. It is larger than *C. chrysanthus* (10-13cm/4-5in) with lilac-blue flowers. Bulbs should be planted in midsummer, 10cm (4in) deep |

## CORKSCREW HAZEL
*(Corylus avellana* 'Contorta'*)*

An unusual and decorative tree for containers, the corkscrew hazel is slower growing than the ordinary hazel and will live happily in a large half-barrel for many years. The twisted branches give the plant an oriental appearance, particularly in winter when the outline can be seen most clearly. The yellow catkins which appear this month are particularly attractive, dangling from the branches and being blown about in the wind.

| type | Deciduous shrub or small tree |
| --- | --- |
| flowers | Yellow catkins in late winter |
| height | 2.5m (8ft) |
| spread | 2m (6ft) |
| planting | Mid-autumn to early spring; choose a specimen about 45cm (18in) high and plant in a large pot. Transplant to half-barrel in second year |
| site | Sun or partial shade |
| compost | Loam-based |
| care | Feed established specimens monthly with a liquid feed from early spring to late summer. Water well in dry spells. In early years of growth, prune the previous year's shoots back by a half to encourage bushy growth |
| propagation | From seed sown in mid- to late autumn or by pegging down layers, also in autumn |

# *practical* project

## MAKING AN ALPINE TROUGH GARDEN

Old stone sinks and troughs that were originally used in farmyards and dairies make attractive containers for alpine species and smaller rock plants. They are extremely heavy, especially when planted up, so are not really suitable for rooftop or balcony sites. However, given an open, sunny position, they can be sited just about anywhere else – on a patio, in a paved courtyard or just under a kitchen window.

The problem is that genuine stone troughs are rare and nowadays tend to be found only in expensive antique shops. Fortunately, reconstituted stone versions are available which are far cheaper. You can also still pick up old ceramic 'butler' sinks which can be adapted for alpine growing.

### TRANSFORMING A CERAMIC SINK INTO A 'STONE' TROUGH

■ Scrub the sink out thoroughly. Rinse and dry.

■ Paint the outer and inner surfaces with a strong adhesive (impact-bonding PVA or similar) and leave to go tacky.

■ Prepare the 'coating'. Use an old wooden board as the mixing surface and mix together two spadefuls of peat or peat substitute (finely sieved), one spadeful of builder's sand and one spadeful of cement, adding enough water to make a stiff consistency.

■ Apply the coating (approximately 2cm (¾in) thick) to the sink with a builder's trowel, or by hand (wearing gloves) if you find it easier. Work quickly, as the mixture tends to harden after about three-quarters of an hour. Cover the outside completely – the inside only needs

to be coated to below the final level of the compost. Don't make the surface too smooth: it should look like roughened stone.

■ Protect the trough from rain for four or five days until the coating is set completely.

### PLANTING A SINK OR TROUGH

■ Cover the plug hole with a piece of wire mesh or broken crocks.

■ Add a 10cm (4in) layer of coarse grit, gravel or stone chippings (avoid limestone chippings if planting lime-haters).

■ Half-fill the trough with a moist, gritty compost (two-thirds loam-based potting compost; one-third grit, gravel or small stone chippings).

■ Place one or two stones or rocks in the compost and continue to add more compost, so that they are naturally 'bedded' in the trough.

■ Position the plants on the surface of the compost (still in their pots) and move them around until you are satisfied with the arrangement. Resist the temptation to overplant the trough and leave enough space for each plant to grow to its full size.

■ Make planting holes, remove the plants from their pots and place them in the holes. Add more compost if necessary and firm in the plants.

■ Water thoroughly, using a can with a fine rose so as not to disturb the surface, and finish with a 2.5cm (1in) layer of gravel or stone chippings.

### SITING THE TROUGH

Choose a position away from overhanging trees, where the trough will receive sun for at least half the day. Raise the trough off the ground slightly to help drainage – use bricks, but take care not to block the drainage hole.

## CHOOSING ALPINE PLANTS FOR CONTAINERS

The aim is to choose small, compact, slow-growing species that will not swamp the trough and can be left in position for many years. Larger troughs can include dwarf conifers and all troughs can incorporate some miniature bulbs. Alpine enthusiasts may like to use a trough to grow a collection of one genus of plants, such as gentians or primulas.

| plant | height | spread | description |
|---|---|---|---|
| **DWARF CONIFERS** | | | |
| *Chamaecyparis pisifera* 'Nana' | | | |
| | 45cm (18in) | 45cm (18in) | bushy |
| *Juniperus communis* 'Compressa' | | | |
| | 60cm (2ft) | 15cm (6in) | upright |
| *Thuja occidentalis* 'Caespitosa' | | | |
| | 30cm (12in) | 30cm (12in) | rounded |

*COMPOST FOR ACID-LOVERS*
For acid-loving alpines use a specially prepared ericaceous potting compost, mixed with one-third grit, gravel, sandstone or granite chippings (avoid limestone).

*ALTERNATIVE CONTAINERS*
Alpine growing does not have to be confined to troughs and sinks, although this is the traditional way of growing these plants. Terracotta pots, shallow alpine 'pans', old chimney pots (see p.96) and strawberry planters (pp.76–7) are also suitable, as long as the correct compost is used and good drainage is provided.

*(Continued on page 26)*

# *practical* project

## MAKING AN ALPINE TROUGH GARDEN

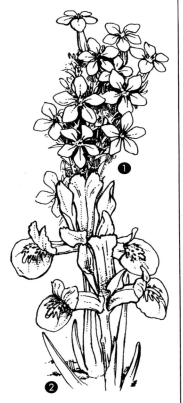

## CHOOSING ALPINE PLANTS FOR CONTAINERS

| plant | height | spread | description |
|---|---|---|---|
| **MINIATURE BULBS** | | | |
| *Crocus imperati* | 10cm (4in) | – | winter flowering; purple |
| *Crocus kotschyanus* | 7.5cm (3in) | – | autumn flowering; lilac-blue with orange spots |
| *Crocus minimus* | 5cm (2in) | – | spring flowering; yellow, marked with purple |
| *Iris histrioides* 'Major' | 10cm (4in) | – | winter flowering; royal blue |
| *Iris pumila* | 10cm (4in) | – | mid-spring flowering; white, purple or yellow (rhizome) |
| *Iris reticulata* | 15cm (6in) | – | late winter/early spring flowering; blue-purple |
| *Sternbergia lutea* | 15cm (6in) | – | autumn flowering; yellow |
| **ALPINES** | | | |
| *Armeria caespitosa* 'Bevan's Variety' | 7.5cm (3in) | 45cm (18in) | early summer; bright pink |
| *Dianthus alpinus* | 10cm (4in) | 15cm (6in) | summer; pale pink to purple |
| *Dianthus deltoides* | 15cm (6in) | 15cm (6in) | summer; pink, red or white |
| *Dianthus neglectus* | 15cm (6in) | 15cm (6in) | summer; pale pink to crimson |
| *Frankenia thymaefolia* | 5cm (2in) | 45cm (18in) | summer; pink |

| plant | height | spread | description |
|---|---|---|---|
| *Gentiana acaulis* | | | |
| | 7.5cm (3in) | 30cm (12in) | early summer; deep blue |
| *Gentiana saxosa* | | | |
| | 10cm (4in) | 15cm (6in) | late summer; white (acid-lover) |
| *Gentiana verna* 'Angulosa' | | | |
| | 7.5cm (3in) | 15cm (6in) | late spring; blue |
| *Geranium dalmaticum* 'Album' | | | |
| | 7.5cm (3in) | 30cm (12in) | summer; white |
| *Helianthemum alpestre* | | | |
| | 10cm (4in) | 30cm (12in) | midsummer; bright yellow |
| *Phlox douglasii* | | | |
| | 7.5cm (3in) | 45cm (18in) | late spring; pale lavender |
| *Phlox subulata* | | | |
| | 7.5cm (3in) | 45cm (18in) | spring; pink or purple |
| *Primula auricula* | | | |
| | 15cm (6in) | 15cm (6in) | spring; yellow or purple |
| *Primula farinosa* | | | |
| | 10cm (4in) | 15cm (6in) | spring; rose-lilac (acid-lover) |
| *Primula marginata* | | | |
| | 10cm (4in) | 23cm (9in) | spring; lavender blue |
| *Saxifraga cochlearis* 'Minor' | | | |
| | 10cm (4in) | 23cm (9in) | midsummer; white |
| *Saxifraga oppositifolia* 'Splendens' | | | |
| | 5cm (2in) | 45cm (18in) | spring; purple |
| *Saxifraga paniculata* 'Lutea' | | | |
| | 15cm (6in) | 30cm (12in) | midsummer; pale yellow |
| *Thymus praecox* | | | |
| | 10cm (4in) | 45cm (18in) | summer; pink or white |
| *Thymus serpyllum* 'Coccineus' | | | |
| | 5cm (2in) | 38cm (15in) | summer; crimson |

1 Dianthus deltoides
2 Iris reticulata
3 Dianthus neglectus
4 Primula farinosa
5 P. marginata
6 Saxifraga cochlearis

# MARCH

This month marks the busiest time of the year for all gardeners, and even if 'garden' means only a few square feet of concrete there is still plenty of scope for sowing and planting. Seeds can be started off now, but if space is limited it is best to wait until next month and buy young plants from garden centres and nurseries.

As the weather improves, this is a good time to look at the framework of the container garden – the trellis or wire supports, the permanent windowboxes and troughs, the balcony rails or balustrades, and check that they are all in good order. Pruning is another useful task to be accomplished this month, particularly of roses and the winter shrubs that have finished flowering, such as winter jasmine and viburnums. This is also the best time for dividing established hardy perennials, just as they move out of winter dormancy into spring growth.

There is no shortage of colour in the early spring as daffodils come into their main season. With literally thousands of varieties to choose from, most of which can be grown in containers, no self-respecting patio or terrace should be without them. The poet's narcissus (Narcissus poeticus) makes a good container subject, with its white outer petals and orange or crimson-edged centre. For windowboxes, the dwarf hoop-petticoat narcissus (Narcissus bulbocodium) has unusual grass-like leaves, and the dainty yellow flowers will not obscure the view. The yellow-and-white theme for spring can be continued with a specimen shrub, such as the white, star-flowered Magnolia stellata.

Frost is the biggest danger at this time of year, as plants have begun their new growth and are all the more susceptible to damage. Avoid overwatering, as a waterlogged soil combined with a sudden drop in temperature can cause freezing around the roots – a sure way to kill plants, and crack terracotta pots.

# tasks
## FOR THE
## *month*

*MULCHING*
*Plants growing in containers dry out very quickly in dry and/or windy weather. Putting down a 2.5-5cm (1-2in) mulch of organic material, such as garden compost or shredded bark, helps retain moisture and also keep down weeds. Water really thoroughly before laying the mulch.*

## CHECKLIST

Divide perennials
Provide support for climbers
Prune shrubs and roses
Plant new and repot established ferns
Sow half-hardy annuals
Pot up cuttings
Take cuttings of fuchsias and pelargoniums

### DIVIDING PERENNIALS

Vigorous-growing perennials such as michaelmas daisies, day lilies, hardy geraniums, achillea and catmint benefit from being lifted and divided every two or three years. Besides being the simplest method of increasing the stock of plants, division of overcrowded clumps keeps plants in good health and promotes better flowering. Perennials that prefer to be left undisturbed include peonies, hellebores and hostas.

■ Lift the clump and pull the plants carefully apart, or separate them with a fork.

■ Cut out the old, woody centre and trim any roots that are damaged.

■ Replant the sections into fresh pots of compost.

### ANNUAL CLIMBERS

Annual climbers such as *Cobaea scandens* or canary creeper *(Tropaeolum peregrinum)* make colourful temporary screens for

summer, and are light enough to be grown on a free-standing structure. A wooden trough or deep windowbox can be easily adapted by screwing strong wooden uprights into either end. Stretch a length of plastic-coated or wire mesh across and nail securely into the uprights. A more permanent structure can be made by substituting trellis panelling for the mesh.

### SUPPORTING CLIMBERS

Permanent climbers generally need to be planted against a wall or fence and, unless they are self-clinging, will need some kind of support system to keep them in place. Trellis or plastic-coated mesh is best for scrambling and bushy climbers, which can simply be tied in as they grow. Trellis panels come in many different decorative styles and shapes; mesh is measured by the metre (yard). In either case, small

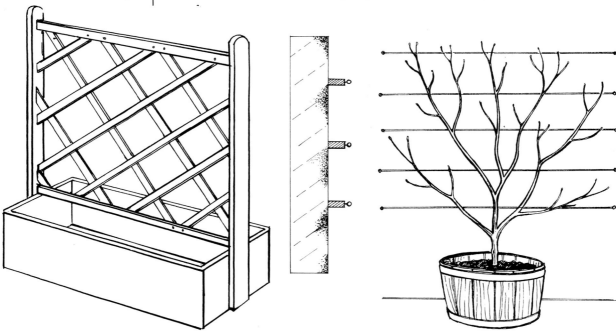

wooden battens should be screwed to the wall or fence first, so as to hold the structure a few centimetres (inches) away and allow air to circulate around the plant stems.

Alternatively, a system of wires can be strung horizontally through vine eyes about 45cm (18in) apart and stretched taut. This is a good method for the more formal training of wisteria and climbing roses, and stems are tied in as they grow.

### PRUNING SHRUBS

Shrubs need to be pruned for a variety of reasons – to control their growth, to remove dead or damaged wood, and to encourage strong new growth and flowers. If they are growing strongly, **winter-** and **spring-flowering shrubs** can all be pruned now (see illustration below).

■ Winter-flowering heather (*Erica carnea*). Trim over lightly to remove the dead flowers.

The following **summer-flowering shrubs** flower on growth made this year, and pruning now encourages the new flowering wood.

■ Santolina, lavender. Clip back all the previous year's growth to points just above the old wood. This needs to be done annually to prevent plants becoming straggly and leggy. Take care not to cut into the old wood.

■ *Buddleia davidii*, caryopteris, hardy fuchsias, (*F. magellanica* and hybrids). Cut back last year's growth to just above the lowest new shoot.

■ *Hydrangea macrophylla*. Cut off the old flowerheads of lacecap and mophead hydrangeas and remove any dead or weak growths.

**Evergreen shrubs** do not require any regular pruning except to remove weak or damaged growth. Exceptions are shrubs like box or privet which are being formally trained, and these are pruned in summer (see p72).

### NOTE

■ *This is the last chance to prune bush roses before new growth begins (see p112)* ■

### FERNS

New ferns can be planted now. Established ferns should have old brown fronds removed, and any that have outgrown their pots should be moved on into pots one size larger. (For details on the care of ferns, see Practical Project, p35)

### SOWING HALF-HARDY ANNUALS

Half-hardy annuals can be raised from seed indoors on a windowsill. The method of sowing is the same as for hardy annuals (see p43). The main difference is that because half-hardy plants need warmth in the early stages of growth, they should not be planted outside until frost danger is over.

### POTTING-UP CUTTINGS

Stem cuttings of shrubs taken last summer (see p73) should now be growing strongly and can be transferred into individual pots. Keep them in light shade and water regularly.

### TAKING FUCHSIA AND PELARGONIUM CUTTINGS

Overwintered plants should now be producing new shoots. Cuttings taken any time between now and late spring will produce flowering plants by the summer. (For cuttings see p51.)

### HALF-HARDY ANNUALS FOR CONTAINERS

**Ageratum**
**French marigold (*Tagetes patula*)**
**Helichrysum bracteatum**
**Mesembryanthemum**
***Phlox drummondii***
**Snapdragon (*Antirrhinum*)**
**Tobacco plant (*Nicotiana*)**

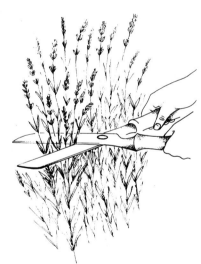

*Clipping lavender*

*Winter jasmine* (Jasminum nudiflorum), *wintersweet* (Chimonanthus praecox). *Cut out one in every three stems.*

# plants
## OF THE
## *month*
## *1*

## CAMELLIA
### *(Camellia japonica)*

One of the best shrubs for container growing, the camellia has year-round glossy foliage and big, showy flowers in late winter and spring. As long as the plant is given some shelter against the wall of the house, the flowers will carry on appearing until the end of spring. The only problem with camellias is that the blooms can be damaged by sun after frost, but this is easily avoided by placing the containers in a position that does not catch the early morning sun.

| | |
|---|---|
| type | Evergreen shrub |
| flowers | White, red or pink; late winter to late spring |
| height | 2m (6ft) |
| spread | 2m (6ft) |
| planting | Autumn or spring |
| site | Light shade; avoid a position in full sun (too hot in summer) and one facing the sunrise (risk of damage from early morning sun after frost). Best on a sheltered patio or in a basement – balconies and roof gardens may be too exposed |
| compost | Lime-free (ericaceous) preferred, although camellias will thrive in a multi-purpose potting compost |
| care | Dead-head after flowering. Keep compost moist but do not allow it to become waterlogged. Apply a surface mulch of leafmould or well-rotted manure in spring |
| propagation | From semi-ripe cuttings in late summer |
| varieties | There are literally hundreds of varieties to choose from including 'C.M. Wilson' with pale pink flowers, 'Bob Hope' with red flowers and 'Alba Simplex' which is pure white |

## ANEMONE
### *(Anemone blanda)*

Anemones are pretty spring flowers for windowboxes and pots, making a welcome change from bulbs. There is a good choice of colours and they are easy to look after.

| | |
|---|---|
| type | Perennial tuber |
| flowers | Pale blue, mauve, pink and white; late winter to mid-spring |
| height | 15cm (6in) |
| spread | 10-15cm (4-6in) |
| planting | plant tubers 5cm (2in) deep in early to mid-autumn |
| site | Sun or partial shade |
| compost | Multi-purpose |
| care | No special care needed |
| propagation | Divide the tubers after the flowers and stems have died back in late summer |
| related species | *Anemone* 'De Caen', the florist's single anemone, is also suitable for containers. It may reach 30cm (12in) high and flowers profusely over several months. *A.* 'St Brigid' is a double form which bears fewer flowers than 'De Caen'. Both types are available in a wide range of colours, including white, pink, magenta, scarlet and blue |

## HYACINTH
### *(Hyacinthus orientalis)*

Hyacinth bulbs can either be planted indoors in bowls to flower in early winter, or outside in pots and windowboxes to give a spring display. Bulbs suitable for indoor flowering have been specially treated, and it is important to check with the garden centre or grower whether you are buying treated or untreated bulbs. The large flowerheads are available in a huge range of colours.

| | |
|---|---|
| type | Bulb |
| flowers | White, blue, cream, yellow, pink, red; spring |
| height | 15-23cm (6-9in) |
| spread | 10cm (4in) |
| planting | For spring flowering, plant untreated bulbs in pots or windowboxes in autumn, 15cm (6in) deep and 15cm (6in) apart (for indoor flowering see p92) |
| site | sunny |
| compost | Multi-purpose |
| care | After flowering, take out the bulbs and replant in a less prominent position if you need the space for summer bedding. Otherwise, leave them untouched to flower again next year |
| propagation | From seed gathered and sown in early summer |
| varieties | There are hundreds of named varieties available: 'Delft Blue' is a powder blue, 'Carnegie' is white, 'City of Harlem' yellow, 'Pink Pearl' is a reliable pink, 'Jan Bos' is the best red |

## DAFFODILS AND NARCISSI

*All daffodil and narcissus bulbs can be grown in containers, although some are more suitable because of their compact size. The typical yellow colour can be varied by using species which are white, cream or varying shades of yellow and orange. By planting a selection of species and named varieties, it is possible to have some narcissus in flower from midwinter right through to spring.*

### CYCLAMINEUS NARCISSUS
#### *(Narcissus cyclamineus)*

| | |
|---|---|
| height | 15-20cm (6-8in) |
| flowers | Deep yellow, pendent heads, 5cm (2in) trumpets, petals swept upwards and backwards; late winter and early spring |
| leaves | Dark green, linear |
| varieties | 'February Gold' – very early, 'Tête-à-Tête' – short cup, 'Peeping Tom' – bright yellow |

### HOOP-PETTICOAT NARCISSUS
#### *(N. bulbocodium)*

| | |
|---|---|
| height | 5-15cm (2-6in) |
| flowers | All-yellow, 2.5cm (1in) trumpets; late winter and early spring |
| leaves | Narrow, cylindrical, grass-like |

### JONQUIL NARCISSUS *(N. jonquilla)*

| | |
|---|---|
| height | 30cm (12in) |
| flowers | Deep yellow, wide petals, small central cup, scented; mid-spring |
| leaves | Cylindrical |

### POET'S NARCISSUS *(N. poeticus)*

| | |
|---|---|
| height | 38-45cm (15-18in) |
| flowers | White, with red central cup; mid-spring |
| leaves | Narrow, strap-shaped |
| varieties | 'Old Pheasant's Eye' – late flowering, deep red 'eye' |

### TAZETTA NARCISSUS *(N. tazetta)*

| | |
|---|---|
| height | 30-45cm (12-18in) |
| flowers | White or yellow petals with yellow central cups; midwinter to early spring. *Note:* may not be hardy in all areas (can be grown indoors, see p92) |
| leaves | Strap-shaped |
| varieties | 'Paper White' – least hardy, 'Soleil d'Or' – orange central cup, 'Minnow' – up to four flowers per stem |

### CULTIVATION
#### *of daffodils and narcissi*

| | |
|---|---|
| planting | Early autumn, 7.5-15cm (3-6in) apart depending on size of bulb, 15cm (6in) deep |
| site | Sun or light shade; pots, windowboxes, troughs |
| compost | Well-drained, multi-purpose |
| care | Allow foliage to die back naturally, as this feeds the bulbs for next year. Alternatively, lift the bulbs when the leaves have turned yellow, but have not died down completely. Store them in a dry place for replanting in the autumn |
| propagation | Every three years, lift the bulbs (as above) and divide any that can easily be separated. Remove offsets and replant both offsets and full-sized bulbs immediately in suitably sized pots |

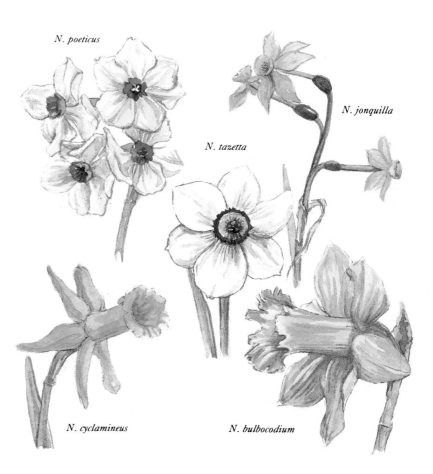

*N. poeticus*

*N. jonquilla*

*N. tazetta*

*N. cyclamineus*

*N. bulbocodium*

# *practical*
# project

## PLANTING FERNS
## IN CONTAINERS

*GOOD COMPANIONS*
*Ferns can be combined with other plants for a more varied effect. Choose those that like similar cool, shady conditions such as hostas, foxgloves, trilliums or lily-of-the-valley.*

Gardeners are often wary of planting ferns, perhaps thinking that they are specialist plants needing expertise and special care. In fact, they are easy to grow, particularly in containers where they can be given a cool, moist environment which might not be possible in open garden borders. They are especially suited to town gardens, where they can fill the damp, shady corners that other plants would shun.

The main difference between ferns and other garden plants lies in the way they reproduce: instead of seeds they have spores, which are carried in capsules on the underside of the leaf or frond. These capsules are arranged in clusters, forming a unique pattern which is used by experts to distinguish one species from another. There is a huge range of species to choose from, but all those mentioned here are hardy and suitable for outdoor growing.

### BUYING FERNS

Garden centres usually offer a small selection of ferns, but check that they are not indoor species which have just been put outside for the summer. Be wary of the commonly sold 'male' fern (*Dryopteris filix-mas*) and 'lady' fern

(*Athyrium filix-femina*) which are too vigorous for containers (although smaller varieties of these species are available: see table). For the widest choice of plants, buy from a specialist nursery (see Useful Addresses) who will also give advice on cultivation.

### BASIC RULES OF FERN GROWING

■ Ferns do not like to dry out, so choose the largest pot available and keep the compost moist. (A few ferns will tolerate dry conditions: see table, p.36.)

■ The plants have very fine, shallow root systems which do not appreciate disturbance. Only repot in spring and early summer, when they are ready to grow vigorously and will adapt most easily to the change.

■ Choose a shady position sheltered from winds – sun and wind will turn the fronds brown (note the exceptions to this rule in the table).

■ Use a loam-based potting compost enriched (if possible) with humus or organic matter – ideally leaf mould or peat substitute.

■ Mulch the top of the pot or trough with gravel, leaf mould or chopped bark to keep the surface roots cool and retain moisture in the compost.

### PLANTING A FERN TROUGH

Any large container can be planted up with ferns, but an antique stone or leaded trough makes a suitably 'period' setting for the plants. The trough will be heavy when full, so put it in position before planting, remembering to choose a shaded, sheltered site. Stand the container on bricks to raise it off the ground and allow the water to drain away freely. Check that there are sufficient drainage holes in the bottom. Water the new plants thoroughly before planting.

■ Cover the drainage holes with broken crocks and add a layer of specially bought clay pebbles or gravel.

■ Mix a loam-based potting compost with some well-rotted leafmould (if available) and add a layer to the trough.

■ Place the ferns in position, allowing room for

*WHAT TO LOOK FOR WHEN BUYING FERNS*

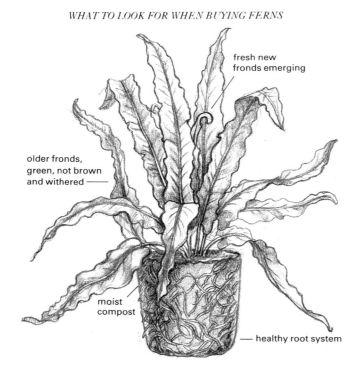

fresh new fronds emerging

older fronds, green, not brown and withered

moist compost

healthy root system

them to develop to their full size (this will vary according to the species and variety – check the table on p36). Top up the trough with the compost and leafmould mix.

- Water well and finish with a top layer of gravel or chopped bark.

## CARE AND MAINTENANCE OF CONTAINER-GROWN FERNS

### Watering
Lightly spray the plants frequently to moisten the top few centimetres (inches) of soil. This is better than soaking the plants with a hose, which can wash the soil away from the delicate roots. It is particularly important to water when the ferns are newly planted and in long hot, dry spells.

### Feeding
Newly planted ferns in fresh compost should not need feeding for the first couple of months. After this, use a general slow-release fertiliser, available as spikes or pellets which can be pushed down into the soil. Take care not to allow any fertiliser to touch the fronds themselves.

### Mulching
This is particularly important for ferns in order to retain moisture around the roots and keep them cool. A 2.5cm (1in) layer of gravel or chopped bark makes an effective mulch, but leaf mould or well-rotted garden compost will add nutrients as well.

### Weeding
Pull up weeds by hand as soon as they appear. Do not use a trowel, which could disturb the roots.

### Pruning
Ferns should only be cut back in spring. The fronds that turn brown in autumn should be left on the plant to protect the crown through the winter. In spring, snip off the old fronds with a pair of sharp secateurs, taking care not to damage any new fronds which may be just about to unfurl.

### Repotting
This should only be done in spring or early summer. Water the plant well and, using a trowel, dig gently around it to lift the entire mat of roots. Replant immediately to the same depth, water thoroughly and add a layer of mulch.

*PLANTING A FERN TROUGH*

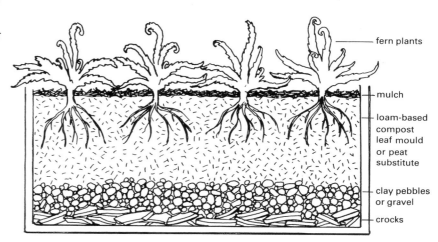

- fern plants
- mulch
- loam-based compost leaf mould or peat substitute
- clay pebbles or gravel
- crocks

## FERN CALENDAR

### SPRING
New fronds unfurling
Plant new ferns
Prune established ferns
Mulch surface of pots

### SUMMER
New fronds fully grown
Mulch surface of pots
Keep compost moist
Remove self-seeded weeds by hand

### AUTUMN
Fronds turn colour

### WINTER
Fronds die back
Move deciduous species out of sight
Display evergreens

## FERN FACTS

Over 10,000 species worldwide

Most are deciduous, dying back after the first frosts. A few, like the spleenwort *(Asplenium trichomanes)* and the common polypody *(Polypodium vulgare)*, are evergreen

Sizes range from the tiny wall rue *(Asplenium rutamuria)* which is 5cm (2in) high, to great tree ferns of 10m (30ft) or more

Ferns (like lichen) are good indicators of air quality, often returning to grow in places once pollution levels are reduced

In Britain, the greatest fern craze was in the Victorian era, when specimens were dug up from all over the world to grace the conservatories and ferneries of grand houses

## *practical* project

### PLANTING FERNS
### IN CONTAINERS

## FERNS FOR CONTAINERS

**Dwarf** *for small troughs/shallow pots*

| plant | size | site | soil |
|---|---|---|---|
| BLACK SPLEENWORT E | | | |
| *(Asplenium adiantum-nigra* | 15-40cm (6-16in) | Sun | Tolerates lime; dry |
| COMMON POLYPODY D | | | |
| *(Polypodium vulgare)* | 15-40cm (6-16in) | Shade | Any |
| COMMON SPLEENWORT E | | | |
| *(Asplenium trichomanes)* | 10-40cm (4-16in) | Sun/shade | Tolerates lime; dry |
| DWARF LADY FERN D | | | |
| *(Athyrium filix-femina* 'Congestum') | 15cm (6in) | Light shade | Neutral to acid; moist |
| DWARF SOFT-SHIELD E | | | |
| *(Polystichum setiferum* 'Congestum') | 15-18cm (6-7in) | Shade | Any |
| RUSTY-BACK FERN E | | | |
| *(Asplenium ceterach)* | 5-15cm (2-6in) | Sun | Tolerates lime; dry |

**Average** *for individual pots/large troughs*

| plant | size | site | soil |
|---|---|---|---|
| AMERICAN MAIDENHAIR E | | | |
| *(Adiantum pedatum)* | 30-45cm (12-18in) | Shade | Neutral to acid; moist |
| AUTUMN FERN D | | | |
| *(Dryopteris erthrosora)* | 20-50cm (8-20in) | Light shade | Any; well-drained |
| CHRISTMAS FERN E | | | |
| *(Polystichum acrostichoides)* | 25-90cm (10-36in) | Shade | Neutral to acid; moist |
| DWARF MALE FERN D | | | |
| *(Dryopteris filix-mas* 'Crispa') | 30cm (12in) | Light shade | Any |
| HART'S TONGUE E | | | |
| *(Asplenium scolopendrium)* | 23-60cm (9-24in) | Shade | Tolerates lime; moist |
| SOFT-SHIELD FERN E | | | |
| *(Polystichum setiferum)* | 30-60cm (12-24in) | Shade | Any; well-drained |

E= Evergreen    D = Deciduous

*American maidenhair*

*Soft-shield*

*Hart's tongue*

*Maidenhair spleenwort*

*Common polybody*

# plants
## OF THE
## *month*
## 2

### AUBRETIA
#### (*Aubretia deltoidea*)

This colourful mat-forming species is already gracing low stone walls and rock banks in the garden at this time of the year, but equally it can be grown in containers. The unseasonally rich mauves and purples make a welcome change from the usual spring yellows. Aubretia is an easy subject for large troughs, tubs and pots as long as it has a well-drained compost, ideally with added lime or limestone chippings.

| | |
|---|---|
| type | Evergreen perennial |
| flowers | Purple, lilac, mauve; early spring to early summer |
| height | 40cm (4in) |
| spread | To 60cm (2ft) |
| planting | Plant in early autumn or early spring. Add a layer of limestone chippings to the base of the container |
| site | Full sun; large troughs, sinks, barrels, pots |
| compost | Loam-based potting compost or alpine mix (see p20) |
| care | Trim back flowering stems after flowering. Insert slow-release fertiliser pellets in late spring |
| propagation | From cuttings taken in late summer |
| varieties | There are many named varieties but for all-year-round interest choose 'Aurea' with gold-edged leaves or 'Variegata' with white-edged leaves |

### BERGENIA
#### (*Bergenia cordifolia*)

These large-leaved plants are useful container subjects, with their evergreen foliage, hardy temperaments and early flowers. They gradually form a pleasing, rounded clump of thickly textured, glossy leaves and need little in the way of nurturing. The pink-purple flowers are held on short, sturdy stems in clusters above the leaves for a month or more in spring and some varieties have the added bonus of winter leaf colouring.

| | |
|---|---|
| type | Evergeen perennial |
| flowers | Rose-pink to purple; early to mid-spring |
| height | 30cm (12in) |
| spread | To 40cm (16in) |
| planting | Mid-autumn to early spring |
| site | Full sun or partial shade; singly in pots or as cover around the base of larger shrubs or trees in barrels |
| compost | Multi-purpose |
| care | No special care needed; can be left indisturbed for several years |
| propagation | Lift and divide clumps in autumn or spring and replant sections immediately |
| varieties | *Bergenia cordifolia purpurea* has leaves flushed with purple in winter. Garden hybrids include 'Abendglut' which has deep red winter foliage and rosy-pink flowers |
| related species | Other bergenias suited to container growing include *B. crassifolia* with pale pink flowers and the smaller leaved *B. stracheyi* which has pale pink or white flowers |

### CHIONODOXA
#### (*Chionodoxa luciliae*)

Often known by their common name of 'Glory of the Snow', chionodoxa are hardy, early spring-flowering plants, which are not deterred by fierce weather. Bulbs planted in the autumn will give a pretty spring display with the minimum of effort. The blue, star-shaped flowers look as if they belong in an alpine meadow, but in fact the plant is easy to care for and does not need the special growing conditions of true alpines.

| | |
|---|---|
| type | Bulb |
| flowers | Light blue with white centres; late winter to early spring |
| height | 15cm (6in) |
| spread | 10cm (4in) |
| planting | Plant bulbs in autumn, 5–7.5cm (2–3in) deep and 10cm (4in) apart |
| site | Full sun; in pots, alpine troughs and windowboxes |
| compost | Well-drained, multi-purpose |
| care | If the space is required for other plants, lift bulbs as the foliage is dying down. Otherwise leave in position until the plants become overcrowded |
| propagation | Lift and divide overcrowded clumps as the leaves are dying back, usually in late spring or early summer |
| varieties | 'Alba' has white flowers and 'Rosea' is a pink form |
| related species | *Chionodoxa gigantea* is a slightly taller version, reaching 20cm (8in). *C. gigantea's* lilac-blue flowers are 4cm (1½in) across. |

## PRIMULA

*Primula is a huge genus of spring-flowering plants, ranging from the simple pale yellow wild primrose* (Primula vulgaris) *to the ruby coloured drumstick primulas* (Primula denticulata) *and encompassing a wide range of alpine and specialist species along the way. Happily for the container gardener, most are suited to growing in pots, window boxes, hanging baskets and troughs. The species fall into a number of groups, each with slightly different growing requirements.*

### ALPINE PRIMULAS

| | |
|---|---|
| type | Hardy perennial |
| flowers | Purple, yellow, lilac, lavender, rose-pink |
| height | 5-15cm (2-6in) |
| spread | 15-23cm (6-9in) |
| planting | Early autumn or early spring |
| site | Full sun or light shade; avoid overhanging trees; in alpine pans, strawberry pots, troughs, sinks |
| compost | Well-drained alpine mix (see p20) |
| care | Move pots to a position that will be sheltered from rain in autumn and winter. Excessive water can damage leaves |
| propagation | From cuttings taken in late summer |
| recommended species | *Primula auricula, P. farinosa, P. marginata* |

### DRUMSTICK PRIMULAS
*(Primula denticulata)*

| | |
|---|---|
| type | Perennial (often grown as a bedding annual) |
| flowers | Held upright above the leaves. Lilac, purple, mauve, rose-pink, white; spring |
| height | 30cm (12in) |
| spread | 23cm (9in) |
| planting | Autumn or early spring |
| site | Full sun or light shade; in pots, window boxes |
| compost | Multi-purpose |
| care | Keep compost moist, particularly in hot, dry spells. If used as spring bedding, remove the plants after flowering to make way for summer bulbs or annuals |
| propagation | Divide after flowering and replant immediately |

| | |
|---|---|
| varieties | 'Alba' is the pure white form; other varieties are in shades of pink, lilac and purple |

### POLYANTHUS

A group of garden hybrids derived from the wild primrose, but in a wide range of colours.

| | |
|---|---|
| type | Hardy perennial |
| flowers | Red, yellow, cream, white, pink, blue; spring, but often sown for winter flowering |
| height | 20-30cm (8-12in) |
| spread | 20cm (8in) |
| planting | Plant mid-autumn or early spring as available |
| site | Full sun or light shade; in pots, window boxes, hanging baskets, wall pots |
| compost | Multi-purpose |
| care | Keep compost moist during dry spells. If used as winter or spring bedding, remove from containers in late spring |
| propagation | Sow seeds in early summer or early autumn in a cold frame. Keep shaded from the sun. Plant out in autumn or spring as required |
| garden hybrids | F1 Rainbow Mixed, Crescendo F1 and Spring Rainbow F1 are all winter hardy mixtures |

### PRIMROSE
*(Primula vulgaris)*

The pretty native primrose deserves a place on any patio. Several coloured hybrids are now also available.

| | |
|---|---|
| type | Hardy perennial |
| flowers | Yellow; spring (coloured hybrids available) |
| height | 15cm (6in) |
| spread | 23cm (9in) |
| planting | Plant between mid-autumn and early spring |
| site | Sun or light shade; in pots, window boxes, wall pots |
| compost | Multi-purpose; moist |
| care | Keep compost moist in dry weather. Mulch with garden compost to retain moisture |
| propagation | Divide after flowering and replant immediately in moist compost |
| garden hybrids | Finesse F1 is a mixture of crimson, purple, rose and blue flowers with silver or gold edging |

# APRIL

The weather may still be unpredictable, but this is not the time for
a slow-down in gardening activity. In fact, this is one of the
busiest periods in the container gardener's calendar, with a range
of jobs begging to be done – not least dealing with the surprising
number of weed seedlings that find their way into the top layer
of compost in larger tubs.

But it shouldn't all be hard work. One of the most pleasurable
tasks for spring is visiting nurseries and garden centres to build
up a collection of plants. These can turn out to be very expensive
outings unless you brace yourself to resist the temptations of large,
mature shrubs and luxuriant climbers in full flower. Better to
build the collection gradually – the seed carousel may not look as
enticing, but annual flowers, herbs, tomatoes and courgettes sown
this month will give you a guaranteed bounty later in the summer,
at a fraction of the price. Bedding plants are also starting to
appear, but these are better bought in late spring or early summer
when the danger of frosts has passed.

Trips to the garden centre can be very enlightening even if you buy
nothing at all. Magnolias are in full bloom, with their goblet-
shaped, rose-pink or white flowers, although only the less showy
M. stellata is really suitable for container growing. Take note of
any varieties of camellia that are still in bloom; some have been
flowering since late winter and deserve a place on any patio.

Back home, take stock of the bulb situation – tulips, grape
hyacinths and crown imperials should be giving a good show,
although narcissi are past their best in many areas.

Next month all the bulbs can be lifted and stored to release
pots for summer planting.

# tasks

## FOR THE

## *month*

**SUMMER PLANTS**
**DEPTH OF PLANTING HOLE**

*Lilium* (lilies) 18cm (7in)
*Galtonia* (Summer hyacinth)
**15cm (6in)**
*Agapanthus* (African lily)
**5cm (2in)**

## CHECKLIST

- Pot up newly bought plants
- Repot potbound plants
- Plant summer-flowering bulbs
- Mulch ferns
- Harden-off half-hardy annuals
- Start feeding programme
- Sow seeds of annuals, herbs and vegetables

### POTTING-UP NEW PLANTS

When you get them back from the garden centre or nursery, most plants will need to be planted out into your own containers. The basic instructions for planting a container can be followed, no matter what shape or size it is (see p20 for advice on types of compost to use).

■ Cover the drainage holes with pieces of broken clay or earthenware pots. This prevents the compost from being washed out of the hole but still allows water to drain away.

■ Add a 2.5–5cm (1–2in) layer of 2cm (¾in) stone chippings or clay aggregate pebbles. Limestone chippings are suitable for most plants except lime-haters, like rhododendrons, which prefer the neutral clay pebbles. This layer improves drainage around the roots.

■ Add a layer of compost – the exact depth depends on the size of the root ball. Aim to make the top of the root ball sit 5cm (2in) below the rim of the pot.

■ Water the new plant well before knocking it gently out of its pot. Set it on top of the compost and fill around with more compost, firming down around the sides. Water thoroughly and add a 2.5cm (1in) layer of compost to the top of the pot.

■ Finally, an optional layer of clay aggregate pebbles can be put on the surface to retain moisture and give a neat appearance.

### REPOTTING

When the roots of a plant have completely filled the pot, it should be repotted into a larger-sized container. A plant that shows no sign of new growth in the spring probably needs to be repotted. Water the plant thoroughly beforehand and select a new pot, no more than 5cm (2in) larger in diameter than the original. Pot up as above.

### PLANTING SUMMER BULBS

A range of interesting bulbs can be planted this month for flowering in the summer. Tall-growing lilies, agapanthus and galtonia can be grown in large pots or tubs to make a striking container feature.

Galtonia, also known as summer hyacinth, is a tall, impressive plant that looks rather like a giant, white bluebell and has a subtle perfume.

Agapanthus, sometimes called the African lily, is also a bold plant, with vibrant blue flowerheads. It is a feeding-rooted perennial rather than a true bulb. *Agapanthus* 'Headbourne Hybrids' is a good, hardy variety.

There are literally hundreds of lilies to choose from, but one of the easiest for outdoor cultivation is *Lilium regale* with trumpet-shaped, white flowers, tinged with pink. Plant the bulbs in a multi-purpose potting compost in groups of three. Keep the compost moist, but not wet.

### NOTE

■ *Lilies are normally potted up in autumn, but may still flower if planted early this month (See p116 for full details on growing lilies.)* ■

### MULCHING FERNS

Newly-planted and established ferns benefit from the application of a spring mulch. All kinds of organic material is suitable for the job – leaves or leaf mould, home-made compost or chopped bark. Spread the material all over the surface of the pots in a layer about 2.5cm (1–2in) deep. Not only does this retain the moisture in the compost, but it will also keep the roots cool – particularly important for shallow-rooting ferns. The mulch also adds nutrients to the compost. Gravel can be used as an alternative – although it has no nutrients.

### HARDENING OFF SEEDLINGS

Seeds sown indoors last month on windowsills or in greenhouses need to be acclimatised gradually to the outside world. Move them to a cold frame or a sheltered porch for a week or so before putting them outdoors.

## BASIC FOOD FOR CONTAINER PLANTS

- *Nitrogen (N)*    encourages leaf/foliage growth
- *Phosphorus (P)*  stimulates a healthy root system
- *Potassium (K)*   essential for fruit and flower production

*Proprietary plant foods will contain a balanced mix of these elements plus traces of other minerals such as magnesium and iron. A liquid tomato fertiliser, for example, contains roughly twice as much potassium as nitrogen and is suitable for flowering plants and tomatoes.*

### STARTING A FEEDING PROGRAMME

Plants grown in containers need more regular and more careful feeding than garden-grown plants, because of the limited amount of nutrients available to them in the potting compost. This particularly applies to smaller containers like hanging baskets and windowboxes. As a general rule, fresh potting compost contains enough nutrients for the first few months of a plant's growth. Newly potted plants won't need to be fed until summer, but established plants should be fed now. Remember, the more plants per container and the closer together they are grown, the more food they will need.

#### Choosing fertilisers

- *Granules or powders*
These are either mixed with the compost when potting the plants, sprinkled on the surface of the compost to be watered in, or dissolved in water and applied like a liquid feed. The particular strength of each make varies, but feeding twice a month should be adequate in the growing season.

- *Liquid feed*
This is the most popular way to feed large quantities of container plants, as the feed is applied, diluted, in a watering can or hose-feeder. In the growing season, apply every two to three weeks.

- *Pellets and sticks*
These are specially prepared, controlled-release fertilisers that are inserted into the compost to release their nutrients slowly over several months. Some brands last for up to six months. An average hanging basket needs four spikes or pellets, but check the instructions on the pack.

### SOWING ANNUAL SEEDS

Hardy annual flowers, herbs and tomato plants can all be started off from seed outdoors this month. Use seed trays or individual 10cm (4in) pots filled with a proprietary seed and cutting compost.

- Fill the seed trays or pots with compost. Water thoroughly and allow to drain.

- Sprinkle the seed thinly over the compost and cover with a 1cm (½in) layer of compost.

- Water with a fine rose, taking care not to disturb the seeds.

- If possible, cover the pots or trays with polythene lids (some trays come with their own see-through covers). A makeshift pot cover can be made by cutting a plastic drink bottle in half – leaving the top off to allow some ventilation. A cover like this keeps off the heavy rain, but preserves moisture and warmth.

- When the seedlings are large enough to handle (when they have two or three pairs of leaves), transplant them into individual, small pots and allow to grow on.

- Keep the compost moist and remove any competing weed seedlings.

*AVOID OVERFEEDING*
*Plants should only be fed when they are in active growth – usually from spring to early autumn. Fresh potting compost contains enough slow-acting fertilisers to see the plants through their first 6–8 weeks of growth. Don't add extra nutrients during this time.*

*CAUTION*
*Keep an eye out for any plant showing signs of drought in the spring. Unexpected dry spells or early heatwaves can cause severe stress to container plants. Pay particular attention to plants that are due to be repotted and keep them well watered.*

# plants
## OF THE
# *month*

*SUMMER-FLOWERING
CLEMATIS
Summer-flowering clematis
produce their flowers on the
current season's stems and,
therefore, flower later than
C. montana and C. armandii.
Summer-flowering clematis
include C. 'Barbara Jackman',
which has blue flowers with
magenta strips, C. orientalis,
which has lantern-shaped,
greenish-yellow flowers followed
by feathery seedheads and C.
'Comtesse de Bouchard', which
has bright mauve pink flowers.*

## GRAPE HYACINTH
### *Muscari*

Grape hyacinths are related to *Hyacinthus* and include some 60 species. They are hardy, dwarf plants and look pretty planted around the edge of a container.

| | |
|---|---|
| type | Bulb |
| flowers | Tiny blue to purple flowers in conical heads that look like miniature bunches of grapes; spring |
| height | 15–30cm (6–12in) |
| spread | 10–15cm (4–6in) |
| planting | 7.5cm (3in) deep and 7.5cm (3in) apart, from late summer to late autumn. Mix with other plants or plant in groups |
| site | Full sun. Shade increases leaf growth but reduces flowering |
| compost | Well-drained, multi-purpose |
| care | Water regularly but don't let the soil become over-wet. Apply a liquid feed from time to time during the growing season |
| propagation | By division every three years. Wait until the leaves are yellow before lifting and repot at once |
| recommended species | *Muscari armeniacum* is deep blue with white edges; mid to late spring. *M. botryiodes* is sky blue; early to late spring |

## CLEMATIS
### *Clematis montana*

One of the many clematis species, *C. montana* is a vigorous spring-flowering climber, suitable for large tubs and barrels. It clings by means of tiny leaf stalks and is best supported by a wall or trellis, pergola or post. It is easy to grow and produces masses of flowers.

| | |
|---|---|
| type | Deciduous, vigorous climber |
| flowers | White or pale pink; late spring |
| height | Up to 12m (40ft) |
| spread | Up to 6m (20ft) |
| planting | Singly, mid-autumn to early spring. Set a cane against the young plant for support. Young growth may need tying in |
| site | Sunny spot, but with the roots shaded from the heat. The plant does best on a warm wall |
| compost | Loam-based |
| care | Water well in dry spells. Mulch in spring. Apply a liquid feed once a fortnight during the growing season. Avoid pruning except to remove dead, damaged or straggly stems or to restrict spread. If pruning is needed do this after flowering |
| propagation | By semi-ripe cuttings in mid- to late summer |
| varieties | *Clematis montana* 'Elizabeth' is soft pink; *C. m.* 'Rubens' has bronze-green foliage and pale pink flowers |
| related species | *C. armandii* is an evergreen clematis with scented white flowers in mid-spring |

## TULIP
### *Tulipa*

Tulips are an excellent way of brightening up a patio garden from early to late spring, before the less hardy summer bedding plants are in flower. A huge range of flower shapes and plant sizes is available, including the smaller species like *T. gregii* which is no more than 23cm (9in) high.

| | |
|---|---|
| type | Bulb |
| flowers | All colours; spring to early summer |
| height | 15–60cm (6–24in) |
| spread | 10–20cm (4–8in) |
| planting | In groups of four or more bulbs, 15–30cm (6–12in) deep, 15–30cm (6–12in) apart, late autumn to early winter |
| site | Sunny and sheltered from the wind |
| compost | Well-drained, multi-purpose |
| care | Water regularly, but avoid over-watering. Apply a liquid feed once a fortnight from the appearance of flower buds until one month after the flowers fade. The bulbs can be left in position, but should be lifted and divided every three years |
| propagation | By division. Lift plants when leaves |

start to wither, remove the offsets and store them with the bulbs in a dry place ready for replanting in the autumn

varieties  For container growing try *Tulipa* 'Brilliant Star', a single, early tulip with scarlet blooms; *T. kaufmanniana* has grey-green leaves and is an ideal height for windowboxes

## MAGNOLIA
### *Magnolia stellata*

Magnolias are such a welcome sight in the spring garden but, sadly, few of the species are suitable for container growing. *M. stellata* is the exception – its compact size and form make it perfect as the centrepiece of a large tub.

| | |
|---|---|
| type | Deciduous shrub |
| flowers | White, fragrant, star-shaped; early to mid-spring |
| height | 2.4–3m (8–10ft) |
| spread | 2.4–3m (8–10ft) |
| planting | Early to mid-spring. Support the plant with stakes for the first few years |
| site | Sun or partial shade, sheltered from cold winds |
| compost | Well-drained, ericaceous or multi-purpose |
| care | Water freely in dry spells. Mulch in mid-spring. No pruning necessary |
| propagation | By layering in early to mid-spring or from seed sown in mid-autumn |
| varieties | *Magnolia stellata* 'Royal Star' has larger blooms with more petals |

## CROWN IMPERIAL
### *Fritillaria imperialis*

*F. imperialis* thrives in containers. It has strong foliage and small clumps of pendent, bell-shaped flowers in mid-spring.

| | |
|---|---|
| type | Bulb |
| flowers | Yellow, orange or red; mid-spring |
| height | 60–90cm (2–3ft) |
| spread | 23–38cm (9–15in) |
| planting | Singly, on their sides, so that the hollow crowns do not gather water. Plant 20cm (8in) deep from early to late autumn. Handle the bulbs carefully as they bruise easily |
| site | Full sun or partial shade |
| compost | Well-drained, multi-purpose |
| care | Crown Imperials do best if left undisturbed, so do not transplant for at least four years. Cut down stems to ground level in summer when the plants die off |
| propagation | By removal of offsets after flowering. Replant offsets in individual pots |
| varieties | *Fritillaria imperialis* 'Lutea' is a lemon-yellow variety |

## RHODODENDRON
### *Rhododendron hybrids*

Rhododendron hybrids bred for the small garden are particularly suited to growing in containers because the soil and growing conditions are more easily controlled than in the garden proper.

| | |
|---|---|
| type | Deciduous and evergreen shrubs |
| flowers | Various; spring to early summer |
| height | To 2m (6ft) |
| spread | To 2m (6ft) |
| planting | Singly, or with other plants. Evergreens in spring, deciduous varieties in autumn to late winter |
| site | Dappled or semi-shade. Sheltered from cold winds and protected from exposure to full sun |
| compost | Moist, multi-purpose. Alternatively, use an approved rhododendron or ericaceous potting compost |
| care | Water freely in dry weather, but avoid over-wet soil. Use rainwater instead of tapwater in areas with hard water. Give a liquid feed during the growing season. No pruning necessary |
| propagation | By semi-ripe cuttings in late summer |
| varieties | *R.* 'Hydon Hunter' is a deciduous variety with a neat habit and unusual, red-rimmed flowers; *R.* 'Percy Wiseman' is evergreen with peach-coloured flowers |

*Crown Imperial*

*Rhododendron*

# *practical* project

## MAKING A MINIATURE WATER GARDEN

*ALTERNATIVE CONTAINERS*
*Plastic tubs are practical, watertight and cheap. A large surface area is important, so avoid long, narrow shapes: it should be at least 30cm (12in) deep. Black or brown tubs usually work better than brightly coloured versions, which can detract from the plants. Even a washing-up bowl could be used, planted with a miniature waterlily. Old ceramic sinks also make good water gardens. If the plug has disappeared, buy another and glue it into place with a waterproof adhesive.*

There's no need to give up the idea of growing water plants, just because you don't have a proper pond. Water gardening in containers is relatively simple and, where a full scale pond would be impractical, they provide a realistic alternative. Several types of container are suitable for converting into a miniature pond, as long as they can be made watertight.

### A pond in a barrel

Wooden half-barrels are probably the most attractive choice for your pond. Originally, they were used for storing liquids – cider, beer, wine or brandy – so there's no reason why they shouldn't be made watertight again. The problem is that, having been sawn in half and stored dry, the wood may well have shrunk or split.

### MAKING THE BARREL WATERTIGHT

■ Fill the barrel with water to swell the wood and seal the joints. Keep topping up the water, for a few days if necessary, until it stops leaking out. For barrels in good condition this should be all the treatment that is needed.

■ If the barrel continues to leak, empty out the water and allow the barrel to dry again. Fill the joints with a mastic sealant (used for sealing glass tanks and aquariums and sold at hardware shops or specialist aquatic centres).

■ For barrels in very poor condition it may be necessary to line the barrel with a flexible plastic or butyl rubber pool liner. Choose a black liner and cut to size. Paint a rubber adhesive around the rim and press the liner firmly against the side of the barrel. Alternatively, use a staple gun to fix the liner to the wood.

### PLANTING THE CONTAINER

■ Put the plants into plastic baskets designed for use in pools to make maintenance easier. Choose circular or rectangular baskets according to the shape of the container.

■ Line the basket (if necessary) with a proprietary basket liner. Half fill with aquatic compost (available from water-garden centres).

■ Set the plant in position and fill around the roots with compost, up to 2.5cm (1in) below the rim.

■ Cover the surface with a layer of gravel or stone chippings to prevent the compost being washed into the water.

### Positioning the plants

As with a full-sized pool, different types of plant need to be positioned at different water levels. Pots containing marginal plants that need to be near the surface of the water can be raised on bricks.

### KEEPING THE WATER CLEAR

Add one or two water snails (available from aquatic centres) to every barrel or large container. They will eat any decaying vegetation and keep the water clean. Grow at least one floating-leaved plant, such as water lilies or water hawthorn. These will cover part of the water surface and prevent the build up of blanketweed and algae. Always top up the pool with rainwater rather than mineral-rich tapwater.

---

**NOTE**

■ *Open-weave pool baskets need to be lined before planting to prevent the soil washing out. Close-weave baskets can be planted directly with compost.* ■

---

## MAINTENANCE CALENDAR

### LATE SPRING

*Plant new plants; repot others every two years; divide overgrown clumps of water hawthorn, iris and bog bean*

### SUMMER

*Snip off flowerheads as they die; divide water hyacinths*

### AUTUMN

*Cut back decaying foliage; thin out oxygenators*

### WINTER

*Remove water hyacinths and water milfoil and over-winter in a shallow tank of water in a frost-free place; keep water free of ice*

---

## PLANTS FOR CONTAINER POOLS

### OXYGENATORS
Include one or two bunches of oxygenating plants, such as *Potamogeton crispus*, which can be planted in a small basket at the bottom of the container.

### AQUATICS
**Miniature waterlilies**
*Nymphaea pygmae helvola* – spreads to 30cm (12in), yellow flowers
*Nymphaea* × *marliacea* 'Carnea' – spreads to 60cm (24in), pale pink flowers

**Water hawthorn (*Aponogeton distachyos*)** – spreads to 60cm (24in), white flowers
**Water milfoil (*Myriophyllum aquaticum*)** – spreads to 60cm (24in), attractive light green foliage

### MARGINALS
*Iris kaempferi* – height to 60cm (24in), spreads to 30cm (12in), blue-purple flowers
**Bog bean (*Menyanthes trifoliata*)** – height to 30cm (12in), spreads to 30in (12in), white flowers

### FLOATING PLANTS
**Water hyacinth (*Eichornia crassipes*)** – height to 15cm (6in), spread to 45cm (18in), blue-purple flowers

*Iris kaempferi*

*Water hyacinth*

*Miniature waterlily*

# MAY

As spring drifts into summer and the threat of night frosts recedes, container gardening can begin in earnest. The garden centres and nurseries are packed to capacity with bedding plants – a rather unflattering name for annuals and tender perennials which are not hardy enough to have been planted out before now. Don't be put off by the name: bedding plants are the most economic way to fill large numbers of pots, hanging baskets and windowboxes. They are also one of the few plants you can safely buy from market stalls and roadside sellers, who will be considerably cheaper than the garden centres. Strips of lobelia, antirrhinum, petunia, nicotiana, stocks, verbena, impatiens, French marigolds and nasturtium, combined with the huge range of upright and trailing pelargoniums, provide endless colour and design possibilities. The important thing to remember is that plants packed closely together like this will be greedy for nutrients and water, so daily watering and fortnightly feeding is essential. Snipping off the flowerheads will help prolong the display.

A couple of shrubs are worth a special mention this month. The Mexican Orange (Choisya ternata) has all the qualifications of a near-perfect patio shrub. The species grows to a height of 2m (6ft) although commercially produced hybrids like 'Aztec Pearl' remain a compact 1m (3ft). The foliage is evergreen, glossy and aromatic when crushed between the fingers. The flowers borne this month and again in late summer are sweetly scented. It's an all-round, hard-working, easy-to-care-for plant. A close runner-up in this competition would be Weigela florida 'Variegata' with its arching branches, cream-edged leaves and pale pink flowers. It is deciduous, so never looks its best in winter, but the late spring flowers which last well into summer are irresistible.

# tasks
## FOR THE
## *month*

**BIENNIALS AND PERENNIALS TO SOW**

**BIENNIALS**
Daisy *(Bellis perennis)*
Forget-me-not *(Myosotis)*
Foxglove *(Digitalis)*
Sweet William *(Dianthus barbatus)*
Wallflower *(Cheiranthus)*

**PERENNIALS**
Achillea, Campanula,
*Coreopsis grandiflora*,
Geum, Heuchera,
Oriental poppy *(Papaver orientalis)*

## CHECKLIST

- Lift and store bulbs
- Plant hanging baskets
- Remove spring bedding
- Sow biennials and perennials
- Plant pelargoniums and fuchsias

### LIFTING AND STORING BULBS

With the exception of snowdrops (see p15), spring bulbs can be lifted and stored to release pots for summer planting.

▪ Lift the clumps carefully with a trowel and remove the compost.

▪ Put them in boxes in a well-ventilated place (a shed or outhouse is ideal) and allow the leaves to dry out naturally, so that they can be easily pulled or cut away from the bulbs.

▪ Peel away any dead skins and trim off the roots.

▪ Place the bulbs in boxes or trays or hang them in mesh bags, such as supermarket fruit bags, and store in a cool, dry place.

### REMOVING SPRING BEDDING

Once wallflowers and forget-me-nots have finished flowering, they can be pulled up and discarded to make room for summer bedding plants.

### SOWING HARDY BIENNIAL AND PERENNIAL SEEDS

Biennials sown now will flower next year. Many hardy perennials will also flower the year after sowing, though others may take two years or more. The method of sowing is the same as for annuals (see p43). When

large enough to handle, the seedlings should be transplanted into individual pots and placed in a lightly shaded spot or open cold frame. Biennials will be ready to be moved into their flowering positions by autumn, perennials the following spring.

### GROWING PELARGONIUMS

Probably the most popular of all summer-flowering container plants, pelargoniums (popularly known as geraniums) come in a wide range of colours from vivid scarlet and pink to subtle shades of mauve and deep maroon. Some varieties also have attractively variegated leaves. They are easy to grow, and if given a place in full sun will flower for weeks on end.

Besides the familiar **zonal** pelargoniums, there are also trailing **ivy-leaved** and balcony varieties, which are ideal for hanging baskets, windowboxes and wall containers. The **regal** pelargoniums are richly coloured and showy, most suitable for growing in individual containers or in the centre of a hanging basket.

*STORING BULBS*
*Before storing bulbs for the summer, label the boxes with the name, colour and height of the bulbs, so that you know where to replant them in autumn.*

### NOTE

▪ *Hanging baskets can be planted up now (see this month's Practical Project, pp54-6).* ▪

Grow pelargoniums in a sunny position, using a multi-purpose compost. During the flowering season, water moderately, feed every ten days or so with a high-potassium food such as tomato fertiliser and remove the faded flowers regularly. Pelargoniums are not frost hardy and must be kept in a frost-free place over winter.

### Taking pelargonium cuttings

New plants are easily propagated, and cuttings taken in late spring will produce flowers by summer.

- Choose strong, healthy shoots 7.5-10cm (3-4in) long and trim below a leaf joint.

- Remove all the leaves except for the top one or two, and any flower buds.

- Dip the cut end into hormone rooting powder.

- Insert the cuttings into individual pots of potting compost and keep on a windowsill, uncovered.

- Move them into larger pots when signs of new growth appear.

- Pinch out the growing tips of bush plants when they reach 15cm (6in) high.

### GROWING FUCHSIAS

Half-hardy hybrid fuchsias are popular pot plants, to be placed outside on the patio in summer and overwintered in a frost-free conservatory or porch. Fuchsias are either upright bushes suitable for individual pots and for training as standards, or trailers to be grown in hanging baskets and balcony windowboxes. Colours range from pure white through cream, pink, red and crimson. All have the characteristic dangling flowerheads, where the outer sepals are usually a contrasting colour to the inner petals (see p63 for varieties).

Fuchsias will grow happily in a sheltered, sunny position and should be watered and fed regularly from early summer to early autumn.

### Taking fuchsia cuttings

Cuttings taken in late spring will produce flowers by summer.

- Choose shoots with three or four pairs of leaves and trim off just above lowest pair.

- Dip the ends in hormone rooting powder.

- Insert four or five cuttings around the edge of a 7.5cm (3in) pot filled with seed compost.

- Cover with a plastic bag and keep on a warm windowsill. The cuttings will root within two to three weeks. Once they are growing strongly, move them into individual pots.

- When they are 10-12.5cm (4-5in) high, pinch out the growing tips to encourage bushy growth.

*SCENTED PELARGONIUMS*
*The scented-leaved pelargoniums have attractive and aromatic foliage which more than compensates for their small and simple flowers. Peppermint, rose and lemon-scented varieties are quite happy in a semi-shaded position.*

## TRAINING A STANDARD FUCHSIA

*Standard fuchsias are easy to grow and train from plants raised from cuttings, but for quicker results you can buy small plants of an upright-growing variety such as 'Fascination'.*

- *Insert a cane alongside the stem and tie it in. Keep pinching out the side shoots as they develop.*
- *As the plant outgrows its pot, move it on to a larger size and insert a taller cane.*
- *When the stem has reached the required height, pinch out the growing tip and allow five or six shoots to develop – these will form the standard head. Pinch out any leaves that develop on the main stem.*
- *Give the fuchsia a liquid feed weekly through the summer months, and move into a frost-free place in early autumn.*
- *In subsequent years, trim the head in early spring and repot as needed.*

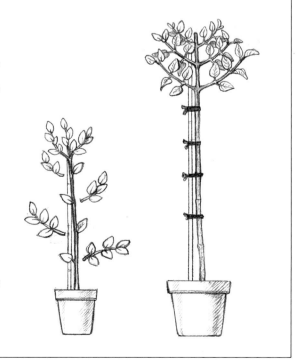

# plants
## OF THE
## *month*

*Rock rose*

### MEXICAN ORANGE
#### *(Choisya ternata)*

The hardiest of the choisyas, this is a good shrub for a sheltered patio or near the house wall, where it will stay evergreen all year round. The flowers look rather like orange blossom, hence the name, and are sweetly scented. In favourable positions there will sometimes be more than one flush, the main one in spring and one or two more later in the summer. The glossy leaves are slightly aromatic.

| | |
|---|---|
| type | Evergreen shrub |
| flowers | White, scented; mid- to late spring and intermittently until early autumn |
| height | 1.5m (5ft) |
| spread | 2m (6ft) |
| planting | Mid- to late spring |
| site | Sunny; against a warm wall or other position where it will be sheltered from wind and frost |
| compost | Multi-purpose or loam-based |
| care | Water in dry spells. In cold winters, bring the shrub into a sheltered porch, or protect with hessian or plastic sheeting. No regular pruning is necessary. Thin out any straggly shoots after the main flowering |
| propagation | By semi-ripe cuttings in late summer |
| varieties | 'Sundance' has golden foliage; 'Aztec Pearl' is more compact, growing to a height and spread of 1-1.2m (3-4ft) – the flowers are pink in bud |

### ROCK ROSE
#### *(Helianthemum nummularium)*

The saucer-shaped flowers of the rock rose provide a blaze of colour throughout the summer. Best known as garden rock plants, they can be grown in containers, where their natural invasiveness will not be a problem.

| | |
|---|---|
| type | Evergreen sub-shrub |
| flowers | Red, yellow, orange, bronze, pink, white; summer |
| height | 15cm (6in) |
| spread | 60cm (2ft) |
| planting | Autumn or spring |
| site | Sunny; in large pots or troughs |
| compost | Well-drained, multi-purpose |
| care | Cut back after flowering to maintain a neat shape. This will induce a later flush of flowers in early autumn |
| propagation | By semi-ripe cuttings in late summer |
| varieties | Many named varieties to choose from, including 'Ben Nevis', a tawny orange and 'Wisley Primrose', yellow |
| related species | There are other species in the group which don't spread quite as widely and are more suitable for an alpine trough or smaller pots. *H. alpestre* has bright yellow flowers and grows to a compact 10cm (4in) high and 30cm (12in) across. *H. lunulatum* is also yellow, but taller at 23cm (9in) |

### LOBELIA
#### *(Lobelia erinus)*

This dwarf, spreading flowering plant is one of the mainstays of summer container planting, trailing over the sides of a wooden barrel or creating a ball of colour in a hanging basket. Compact and trailing varieties are available.

| | |
|---|---|
| type | Annual |
| flowers | Blue, white, deep red; late spring to late summer |
| height | 10-23cm (4-9in) |
| spread | 30cm (12in) or more |
| planting | Late spring |
| site | Sun or partial shade; pots, windowboxes, hanging baskets |
| compost | Multi-purpose |
| care | Water regularly to keep the compost moist. Use a liquid feed every two weeks during the growing season. Discard plants |

when they have finished flowering, usually in early autumn

propagation From seed in mid-spring
varieties *Compact:* 'Cambridge Blue' – pale blue, 'Crystal Palace' – dark blue, 'Snowball' – white
*Trailing:* 'Blue Cascade' – blue, 'Sapphire' – bright blue with a white eye

## WEIGELA
### (Weigela florida)

A popular, easy-care shrub which can be grown with other annuals and perennials while it is still young, but makes a handsome specimen plant for a large tub or barrel when it is fully grown. The arching stems carry pretty pink flowers in late spring and early summer.

type Deciduous shrub
flowers Pink or white; late spring to early summer
height 1.5-2m (5-6ft)
spread 2m (6ft)
planting Autumn or spring
site Sun or partial shade; tubs and large containers
compost Loam-based
care Water young plants in dry spells. Mature plants should be pruned once a year after flowering – cut out one or two of the old stems at ground level

propagation By semi-ripe cuttings in late summer
varieties 'Variegata' is a compact variety with pale pink blooms and cream-edged leaves; 'Candida' is also compact with white flowers; 'Styriaca' has particularly arching branches

## BLUEBELL
### (Scilla non-scripta)

The native English bluebell, once so common in woodlands, can be grown in containers, along with the many garden hybrids of the wild flower. It is particularly suited to growing under deciduous trees or shrubs in large tubs and barrels. Bluebells will tolerate a good deal of shade, particularly during the summer. If you are growing them in less than ideal conditions (in a basement or dark passageway, for instance), try to ensure that the plants get some sunlight through the winter and early spring when the leaves are developing.

type Bulb
flowers Violet-blue (pink and white forms also available); late spring to early summer
height 30cm (12in)
spread 15cm (6in)
planting Plant bulbs in groups in early autumn, 10–15cm (4–6in) deep and 15cm (6in) apart
site In sun or shade. Bluebells prefer some shade from the summer sun, under deciduous trees; in pots, window boxes, tubs and barrels
compost Multi-purpose
care Keep compost moist in hot, dry spells. Leave bulbs undisturbed until overcrowding starts to prevent flowering, then lift and divide the clumps as below
propagation Lift and divide clumps after the foliage has died down. Remove the offsets and replant immediately
garden hybrids Single and mixed colours are available in shades of blue, pink and white
related species *Scilla sibirica*, the Siberian squill, has brilliant blue star-shaped flowers and grows to a height of 15cm (6in); a white form 'Alba' is also available. *S. campanulata* is a popular bulb, growing to a height of 60cm (2ft), with a choice of pink, blue or white

# *practical* project

## PLANTING AND FIXING A HANGING BASKET

*BALANCED BASKETS*
*To stop the basket toppling over during planting, rest it on an empty terracotta flower pot or sturdy bucket.*

*READY-MADE LINERS*
*Ready-made liners have the added advantage that plants can be easily pushed through the slits.*

**KEY**
❶ Card liner
❷ Foam liner
❸ Wire mesh (close)
❹ Wire mesh (wide)
❺ Plastic with drip tray
❻ Traditional wire basket
❼ Half-basket

However little space is available, there is always room for a hanging basket – and there is no better way to create instant colour and greenery to cheer up a bare wall, porch or patio. Late spring is the best time to plant them up, when cheap annual bedding plants are readily available in garden centres. Planted correctly, a hanging basket should go on looking good through all the summer months ahead.

## TYPES OF BASKET

There are two basic types of baskets available: wire and plastic. Coated wire mesh is the most popular because plants can be inserted all the way round the basket to create an overflowing effect. If you want to put in fairly mature plants, choose a wide mesh. This will need to be lined and moisture loss can be a problem; one solution is to place a foil pie dish at the bottom of the basket before planting to hold more water. The alternative is to use solid plastic baskets, which usually have a built-in drip tray. The drawback with plastic containers is that no planting is possible around the sides and it is difficult to disguise the container.

## LINERS

Mesh baskets must be lined to hold the compost inside. Fresh moss, available from garden centres or florists, is the best choice for a natural-looking basket, and plants can easily be pushed through into the compost. A cheaper alternative is to use black polythene, making slits in the surface before planting to allow plants to be pushed through and water to drain out. There are also a range of specially-made liners available in coir fibre, foam and a cotton-based, moss substitute, designed to fit different sizes of basket.

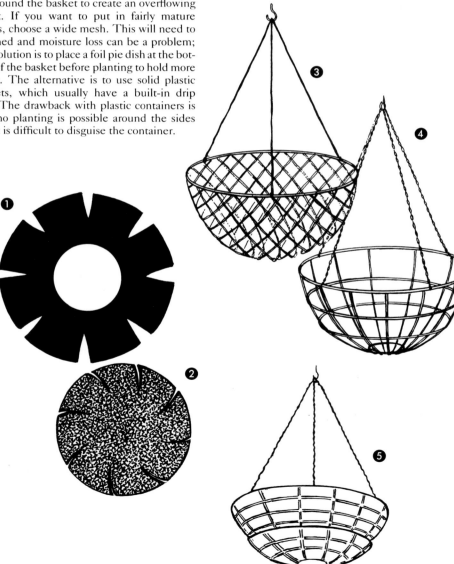

## COMPOST

Any proprietary potting compost can be used for hanging baskets, including those marked specially for containers. If weight is likely to be a problem, choose a peat-based compost or one of the peat substitutes, which are light, although they do tend to be difficult to re-wet once dried out. To help retain moisture, mix some dry water-storing granules with the compost before planting. A small 60gm (2oz) pack is usually enough for six to ten hanging baskets.

## PLANTING

**Using moss**
▪ Line the base and part-way up the sides with fresh moss. Fill the basket one-third full of potting compost.

▪ Add the first layer of trailing plants, working around the base of the basket, pushing the plants through the moss from the outside and anchoring them firmly in the compost.

▪ Add more moss and more compost, and put in a second layer of trailing plants.

▪ Place the upright plants in the centre of the basket, adding more compost as necessary. Do not overcrowd the central area: leave enough room for the root systems to develop.

▪ Water thoroughly and leave to drain before hanging.

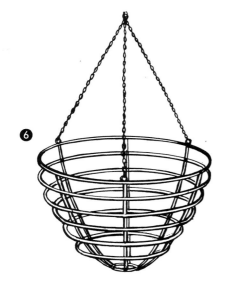

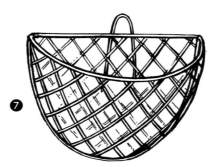

**RECOMMENDED PLANTS FOR HANGING BASKETS**

**TRAILING**
Small-leaved ivy *(Hedera helix)*
Lobelia *(Lobelia erinus)*
Ivy-leaved pelargonium *(Pelargonium peltatum)*
Nasturtium *(Tropaeolum majus* 'Alaska')
*Fuchsia* 'Cascade', 'Falling Stars' or 'Golden Marinka'
*Helichrysum petiolatum*
Verbena *(Verbena × hybrida)*
Trailing helichrysum *(Helichrysum microphyllum)*
Trailing begonia *(Begonia × tuberhybrida* 'Pendula')

**UPRIGHT**
Zonal pelargonium *(Pelargonium × hortorum)*
*Fuchsia* 'Tom Thumb'
Petunia *(Petunia × hybrida,* Grandiflora or Multiflora)
Begonia *(Begonia semperflorens)*
Pansy *(Viola × wittrockiana)*
Busy Lizzie *(Impatiens walleriana)*
Heliotrope *(Heliotropium × hybridum)*
French marigold *(Tagetes patula)*

**COMPACT MOUNDS**
Alyssum *(Lobularia maritima)*
Alyssum 'Gold Dust' *(Alyssum saxatile)*

*MONOCULTURE*
*For real impact, plant each basket with only one type of plant – either in one colour or mixed. A mix of pastel shades of lobelia works well, as does a single-colour pelargonium basket or one full of nasturtiums. Another simple idea is to decorate the front of the house with alternate baskets of variegated and plain ivy. This works well on a formal style of house, where a colourful cottage-garden effect would look out of place. These baskets can, of course, be left in place all year round.*

# *practical* project

## PLANTING AND FIXING A HANGING BASKET

*EASY WATERING*
*Hanging-basket watering devices help to get the water to where it's needed without taking the basket down. Special hose-end fittings are available from garden centres, or make your own by strapping a length of bamboo cane to the end of the hose to make it rigid.*

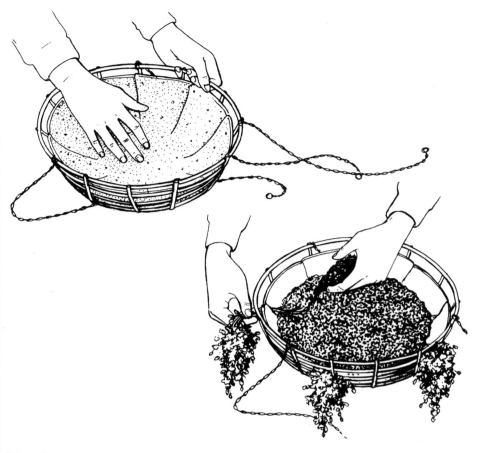

### Using a liner
■ Place the liner in the basket and firm it down well.

■ Plant up in the same way as if using moss, inserting plants through the slits in the liner.

■ Use trailing plants to disguise the liner as they grow.

### FIXING

Baskets must be hung securely, particularly if they are positioned where people will be walking directly underneath them. The best method of fixing is with metal brackets designed for the purpose. These can be bought complete with all the necessary attachments and screws, and come in a range of decorative wrought-iron styles. Generally, they are attached to brickwork or masonry with screws and rawlplugs. Overhead hooks are also available for hanging from wooden porches or verandahs. These should be the heavy-duty variety, with metal plates to prevent the screws from splitting the wood.

### CARE AND MAINTENANCE

Because a large number of plants are sharing a limited amount of compost, they will take up the water and nutrients far quicker than those in large containers. Watering is vital throughout the summer – at first three times a week may be sufficient, but as soon as the dry spell begins, watering will need to be daily, either in the early morning or evening, when there is less risk of scorching the leaves.

A couple of weeks after planting, start to feed with a balanced liquid feed such as a tomato fertiliser. Dilute the feed as directed and apply weekly during the growing season. The alternative is to insert slow-release fertiliser pellets into the compost, which should give enough nutrients for the whole summer. It is best to take down the basket before watering and feeding, allow it to drain and then replace.

# JUNE

Roses take centre stage this month, even though their starring role is all too short. Snipping the heads off the moment they fade will keep the show going as long as possible. There are plenty of other flowers that work just as hard, even if they don't quite have the same glamour. The climbing passion flower, planted against a sunny wall, reveals exotic blooms, one or two at a time – as if it were wary of smothering itself with colour. What the passion flower lacks in daring and scent is more than compensated for by the queen of early summer climbers, the honeysuckle, which fills the summer patio with its perfume and the buzz of insects.

If the weather is hot and dry, the most vital job is watering, closely followed by feeding, as the growing season for most container plants gets into full swing. An evening watering regime is not really a chore and is a good opportunity to see how the plants are faring. A bout of heavy rain can be deceptive, as it often runs off the surface and down the sides of the compost, not reaching the plant roots at all. If watering restrictions are in force, use washing-up and bath water, or install a water butt to collect rainwater.

The plants on a sun-baked patio or warm balcony may wilt in the heat even with regular watering – it is surprising how an early heatwave can put some perennials and bedding plants under stress. The beauty of containers is that they can be moved around to take advantage of shady spots, while shrubby sun-lovers like rosemary and lavender can be left to soak up the rays.

If the weather does not live up to expectations, console yourself with the fact that the summer plants will probably be relieved to have another month to build up roots and foliage before being beckoned into flower by the heat.

# tasks
## FOR THE
## *month*

## CHECKLIST

- Stake tall-growing perennials
- Feed and dead-head roses
- Pot on biennials and perennials
- Prune *Clematis montana*, if necessary
- Put out houseplants and cool conservatory plants
- Start watering programme

### STAKING TALL-GROWING PERENNIALS

Tall-growing perennials often have weak stems that need support, and the earlier in the growing season this is provided the better. Single-stemmed plants like lilies need to be individually staked with bamboo canes, and the stem tied loosely to the cane as it develops. For clump-forming perennials such as phlox, surround the clump with a ring of bamboo canes or interlocking link stakes. As the plants grow they will cover the support.

### ROSE CARE

**Feeding**
Now is the time to give your roses their early summer feed, using a proprietary rose fertiliser (see p125).

**Dead-heading**
Dead-heading roses is an ongoing summer task. It helps the development of strong new growth and, in the case of repeat-flowering roses, encourages the next crop of flowers to follow fast. Cut the stem just above the second or third leaf down. In the case of rose varieties which have ornamental hips in autumn, the flowerheads should be left to allow the hips to develop.

### POTTING ON SEEDLINGS

Biennial and perennial seedlings sown last month will need to be potted on into individual pots or a cold frame. Keep them well watered.

### PRUNING CLEMATIS MONTANA

Although the early flowering *Clematis montana* and *C.macropetala* do not need any regular pruning, if plants

### SWEET PEA SUPPORTS

*In large pots sweet peas can be grown in a variety of attractive ways, either scrambling informally through twiggy sticks or trained up a pyramid of bamboo canes which are lashed together at the top. An alternative method is to grow them through a cylinder of wire or plastic-coated mesh.*

have become too rampant unwanted growth can be cut back this month once flowering is over. Overgrown plants growing in a limited space can have some of the old flowering growth cut out entirely. New shoots should be tied in to the support as they grow.

## PUTTING HOUSEPLANTS OUTSIDE

Some houseplants and conservatory plants will benefit from a spell outside, particularly flowering plants like orchids, azaleas, Christmas cactus, citrus and jasmine. Give them a spot in light shade and keep them well watered.

## WATERING

Container-grown plants dry out rapidly, particularly in hot, dry or windy weather, so watering needs to be carried out at least once a day. The best times to water are in the early morning or evening when it is coolest, so that water is not lost through evaporation and there is less danger of leaf scorch. Always water thoroughly using a fine spray or rose until water comes trickling through the drainage holes at the base of the pot. For large collections of pots, a hose is by far the quickest and most efficient method of watering. It should have a spray nozzle or spray gun attachment to prevent hard jets of water damaging

small plants and displacing soil. For the same reason, watering cans should be fitted with a rose. Long-reach hose lance attachments are particularly useful for windowboxes and hanging baskets.

Micro-drip irrigation systems are available in an easily assembled kit of pipes, drippers and sprinklers. When in place, these apply water where it is needed, directly to the plant roots. They can also be operated with an electronic timer, so are particularly useful for holiday watering.

### Installing a water butt
Where there is space, it is well worth installing a water butt. To maximise water collection, special kits are also available which fit into the down pipe, diverting water from roof guttering to the water butt. In hard-water

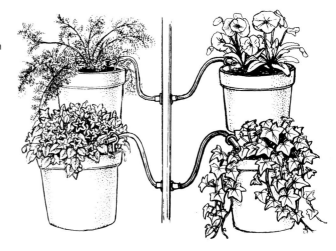

areas where there is a lot of lime in the water, a ready supply of rainwater will be particularly useful for lime-hating plants like camellias and rhododendrons.

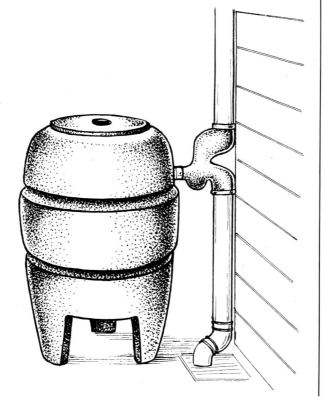

*RETAINING MOISTURE*
*To help retain moisture, water-retaining polymers can be added to the compost in containers. These are crystals which absorb and hold water, supplying it to the plant roots when needed. The crystals should be mixed in with the compost at planting time.*

# plants
## OF THE
## *month*

*Passion flower*

## LILAC
### *(Syringa microphylla)*

A slender, more compact version of the common lilac *(Syringa vulgaris)*, *S. microphylla* is well suited to container growing. The lilac-coloured flowerheads are shorter than those of the common lilac, but are no less fragrant. Flowers appear in two flushes, once in early summer and again in early autumn.

| | |
|---|---|
| type | Deciduous shrub |
| flowers | Lilac, 7.5-10cm (3-4in) long; early summer and early autumn |
| height | 1.2-1.5m (4-5ft) |
| spread | 1.2-1.5m (4-5ft) |
| planting | Autumn |
| site | Sun or partial shade; large tubs or barrels |
| compost | Multi-purpose or loam-based |
| care | No special care needed. Keep watered in long, dry spells. Remove flowers as they fade. In mid-autumn, cut out any weak or crossing branches. Overgrown shrubs in need of rejuvenation can be cut down to 60cm (2ft) above ground level, although flowers will not then appear for two or three years |
| propagation | By semi-ripe cuttings in late summer |
| varieties | 'Superba' is a larger form (up to 2.5m/8ft) with rose-pink flowers |

## COMMON PASSION FLOWER
### *(Passiflora caerulea)*

This vigorous, tender climber, can be grown against a warm wall in milder districts, where it will clothe the brickwork in glossy green leaves and flower profusely. In good years it may even bear fruit. It will need support from a trellis or wires but, despite its tropical looks, needs little in the way of feeding or pampering.

| | |
|---|---|
| type | Evergreen climber |
| flowers | White petals with a corolla of purple-blue filaments and prominent stamens; early summer to early autumn |
| fruits | Oval, yellow/orange |
| height | To 10m (30ft) |
| spread | 2-3m (6-10ft) |
| planting | Late spring; supported with trellis or wires |
| site | Sun or partial shade; against a warm wall |
| compost | Loam-based |
| care | New plants may need to be tied in to supports at first, but should soon start to climb using their tendrils. Mulch the surface of the compost in spring with well-rotted compost or manure. Water regularly during the growing season |
| propagation | By semi-ripe cuttings in late summer |
| related species | The two species grown mainly for their passion fruit, *P. edulis* and *P. quadrangularis*, are not as hardy as *P. caerulea*, and need to be assured a winter temperature of 10°C (50°F). The flowers of *P. edulis* are similar to *P. caerulea*, and *P. quadrangularis* is a deeper purple |

## MOCK ORANGE
### *(Philadelphus microphyllus)*

*P. microphyllus* is a smaller, neater version of the more widely grown garden hybrids. It has the same characteristics – free-flowering and a strong perfume – as its larger cousins *P.* 'Belle Etoile' and 'Virginal'. As the name suggests, all philadelphus have a fragrance reminiscent of orange blossom.

| | |
|---|---|
| type | Deciduous shrub |
| flowers | White, scented; early to midsummer |

| | |
|---|---|
| height | 60-90cm (2-3ft) |
| spread | 60-90cm (2-3ft) |
| planting | Autumn or spring |
| site | Sun or partial shade |
| compost | Well-drained, multi-purpose |
| care | No special care needed. Keep well watered during the growing season and liquid feed once a month. After flowering, cut out any old wood |
| propagation | By hardwood cuttings in autumn |
| garden hybrids | Among the garden hybrids, one or two are sufficiently compact for container growing. 'Avalanche' grows to a maximum height and spread of 1.5m (5ft); 'Sybille' has purple markings on the flowers and grows to a maximum of 1.2m (4ft) |

## FUCHSIA

*Fuchsias are grown mainly for their brightly coloured, pendent flowers which appear in early summer and often last right through until autumn. Both hardy and tender fuchsias can be grown in pots outdoors, although the latter will need to be overwintered in a frost-free place. Upright varieties can be grown as standards (see p51), trailing varieties are particularly suited to hanging baskets. There are even miniature forms which can be planted in windowboxes.*

### HARDY FUCHSIA
*(Fuchsia magellanica)*

The hardiest of all fuchsias, *F. magellanica* will survive mild winters outdoors. It may still be cut down by severe frosts, although it generally recovers and new shoots grow in the spring.

| | |
|---|---|
| type | Deciduous shrub |
| flowers | Crimson, pendent flowers; midsummer to autumn |
| height | 1.2-2m (4-6ft) |
| spread | 60cm-1.2m (2-4ft) |
| planting | Early summer |
| site | Full sun or light shade; pots or tubs |
| compost | Multi-purpose |
| care | Water frequently in dry periods. If frosts are likely, cut the stems down to ground level in late autumn and cover the pot with a layer of peat substitute |

| | |
|---|---|
| propagation | By cuttings in spring |
| varieties | 'Gracilis' has very pretty, slender flowers and narrow leaves; 'Versicolor' has leaves variegated with white and pink markings; 'Pumila' is a miniature variety which grows to about 15cm (6in) high; 'Tom Thumb' is a hybrid which has a height and spread of no more than 30cm (12in) |

### TENDER FUCHSIA
*(Fuchsia hybrids)*

A huge range of tender hybrids are available, all of which are suitable for container growing. Those trained as standards may reach a height of 1m (3ft) by the end of the season; trailing varieties and those grown as small bushes should not exceed 60cm (2ft).

| | |
|---|---|
| planting | Early summer |
| site | Sun or light shade; pots and hanging baskets |
| compost | Loam-based |
| care | Give the plants a liquid feed once a week during the flowering season. Keep well watered until after flowering, then gradually reduce watering until the plants are brought indoors in mid-autumn. Put them in a frost-free place, keeping the compost barely moist. Cut back the stems in late winter (see p21). Repot and place outdoors again in early summer |
| propagation | By cuttings in late spring |
| varieties for hanging baskets | 'Cascade' – white sepals, red petals<br>'Falling Stars' – red<br>'Swingtime' – red sepals and white petals |
| for pots | 'Constellation' – white<br>'Miss California' – pink<br>'Thalia' – red |
| for standards | 'Fascination' – red sepals and rose pink petals |

# *practical*
# project
# 1

## PLANTING AND
## FIXING A
## WINDOWBOX

Most houses and flats have room for one or more windowboxes. The choice of box and the style of planting will depend to some degree on the type of building, as well as on personal preference. Whether you go for a relaxed mix of cottage-garden plants, formal clipped box and evergreens, or cheerful annuals, the scheme can greatly improve the outward appearance of your home. Don't forget that windowboxes are meant to be seen from the inside as well as out, so give some thought to a planting that will look good from all angles.

### CHOOSING THE BOX

The choice is generally between wood, plastic, terracotta and glassfibre boxes, all of which will be light enough for most windowsills. Wooden boxes should be of hardwood or, if they are softwood, should have been treated with a horticultural wood preserver. Although you can plant directly into wooden boxes, it is better to use a plastic liner box which fits snugly inside and prevents the compost coming into contact with the wood. Plastic boxes can also be used on their own – white ones look quite inconspicuous against white paintwork, or choose bold, primary colours like red for a modern setting.

An increasingly common alternative to wood and plastic is glassfibre, which is capable of being moulded into interesting shapes. Imitation leaded windowboxes with decorative relief patterns look attractive and are considerably cheaper and lighter than the real thing.

Whichever type of container you choose, make sure it has drainage holes in the base. It is also useful to have a drip tray to prevent water running on to the sill and possibly staining the paintwork or masonry.

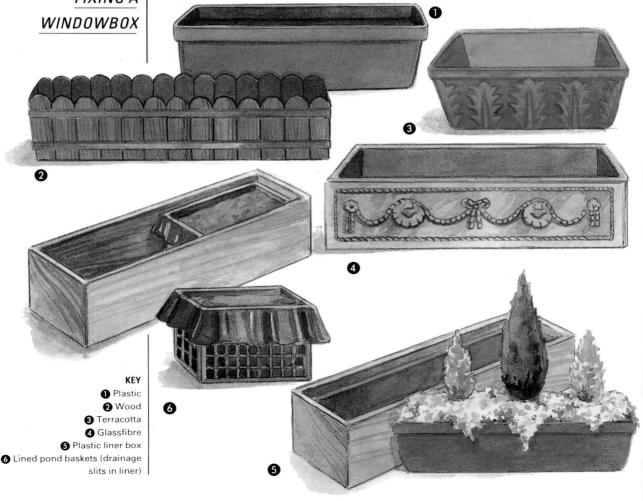

**KEY**
❶ Plastic
❷ Wood
❸ Terracotta
❹ Glassfibre
❺ Plastic liner box
❻ Lined pond baskets (drainage slits in liner)

## PLANTING THE BOX

Do *not* plant a window box *in situ*. It is easier and less dangerous to lift it inside the house or down on to the ground in order to replace plants.

■ Water all plants in their pots before you start.

■ Drill drainage holes in the base if they don't already exist. 2cm (¾in) holes at 15cm (6in) intervals will be sufficient. Cover the holes with pieces of broken clay flowerpot or crocks.

■ Add a 5cm (2in) layer of drainage material: clay aggregate pebbles are light and widely available at garden centres, or alternatively use stone chippings.

■ Cover the drainage layer with multi-purpose potting compost so that the box is just under half full.

■ Start to add the plants, knocking them carefully out of their pots and placing them in position. Trailing plants should be put at the front and sides of the box, upright varieties in the middle.

■ Fill around the rootballs with more compost and firm the plants down to check that they are securely anchored. Water thoroughly and top up with more compost to within 2.5cm (1in) of the top of the box.

## FIXING

There are several ways of fixing a windowbox in position. If the sill is deep enough, the box can simply sit on the sill – although it is a wise precaution to use safety chains and wedges as shown.

If the window has no sill, the box can be attached using brackets – do not use ordinary

*PLANTING A WINDOW BOX*

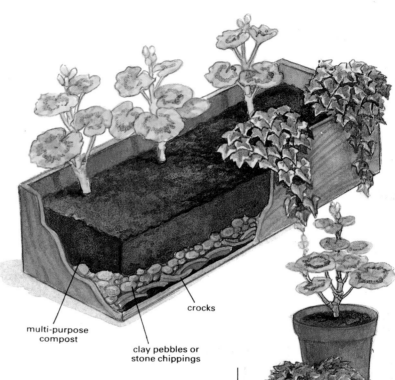

crocks

multi-purpose
compost

clay pebbles or
stone chippings

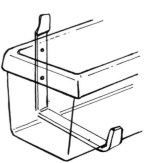

shelf brackets, as the windowbox can easily be knocked off. Garden centres and DIY suppliers sell brackets designed to support plastic and wooden windowboxes: if possible, buy a complete kit with all the fixings and screws. The brackets are fixed to the wall by drilling holes in the màsonry and using rawlplugs and screws. It is not advisable to attach terracotta or large glassfibre boxes using brackets.

Some older houses have cast iron safety rails around the sill which are ideal for keeping windowboxes securely in place.

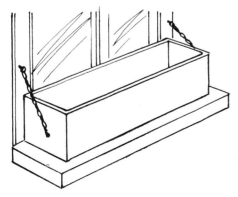

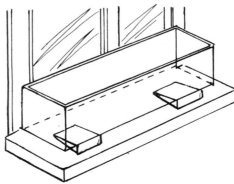

# *practical* project

### PLANTING AND
### FIXING A
### WINDOWBOX

*Anenome and
ivy-leaved pelargonium*

## RECOMMENDED PLANTS FOR WINDOWBOXES

| plant | height | colour | season |
|---|---|---|---|
| **Bulbs** for seasonal colour. Plant in autumn | | | |
| ANEMONE (tuber) | | | |
| *(Anemone blanda)* | *15cm (6in)* | *Blue, pink, mauve, white* | *Spring* |
| AUTUMN CROCUS | | | |
| *(Crocus speciosus)* | *10cm (4in)* | *Lilac-blue* | *Autumn (plant in late summer)* |
| CROCUS | | | |
| *(Crocus chrysanthus)* | *8cm (3in)* | *Yellow, purple* | *Spring* |
| DWARF IRIS | | | |
| *(Iris reticulata)* | *15cm (6in)* | *Blue, mauve, purple* | *Late winter* |
| GRAPE HYACINTH | | | |
| *(Muscari botryoides)* | *15cm (6in)* | *Blue* | *Spring* |
| HYACINTH | | | |
| *(Hyacinthus orientalis)* | *23cm (9in)* | *White, pink, yellow, blue* | *Spring* |
| NARCISSUS | | | |
| 'Peeping Tom' 'Tête à Tête' | *20-30cm (8-12in)* | *Yellow* | *Spring* |
| **Annuals/biennials** – for instant results. Plant in early summer (or when available) as bedding plants from garden centres | | | |
| DAISY (Miniature) | | | |
| *(Bellis perennis* 'Dresden China' *pink)* | *10cm (4in)* | *White, pink, red* | *Summer* |
| DWARF NASTURTIUM | | | |
| *(Tropaeolum majus* 'Alaska' *variegated leaves)* | *25cm (10in)* | *Yellow orange* | *Summer* |
| DWARF WALLFLOWER | | | |
| *(Cheiranthus cheiri* 'Tom Thumb' *mixed)* | *23-30cm (9-12in)* | *White, red Orange, yellow* | *Spring* |
| FRENCH MARIGOLD | | | |
| *(Tagetes patula)* | *30cm (12in)* | *Orange, gold* | *Summer* |
| IVY-LEAVED PELARGONIUM | | | |
| *(Pelargonium peltatum)* | *Trailing to 1m (3ft)* | *Pink, red* | *Summer* |

| plant | height | colour | season |
|---|---|---|---|
| **LOBELIA** | | | |
| (*Lobelia erinus*) | 10-23cm (4-9in) | Blue | Summer |
| **PANSIES** | | | |
| (*Viola × wittrockiana*) | 15cm (6in) | Purple, yellow, blue | Winter and summer |

**Perennials** – for an easy-care, long-lasting display

| plant | height | colour | season |
|---|---|---|---|
| **AUBRETIA** | | | |
| (*Aubretia deltoidea*) | 10cm (4in) | Purple, lilac | Spring |
| **BELLFLOWER** | | | |
| (*Campanula carpatica*) | 23cm (9in) | Blue, purple | Summer |
| **CATMINT** | | | |
| (*Nepeta × faassenii*) | 30cm (12in) | Blue | Summer |
| **LESSER PERIWINKLE** | | | |
| (*Vinca minor*) | 10cm (4in) | Blue, purple | Summer |

**Shrubs and evergreens** – for structure and year-round interest

| plant | height | colour | season |
|---|---|---|---|
| **DWARF BOX** | | | |
| (*Buxus sempervirens* 'Suffruticosa') | 30cm (12in) | | Evergreen |
| **DWARF CYPRESS** | | | |
| (*Chamaecyparis obtusa* 'Nana Compacta') | 60-90cm (2-3ft) | | Evergreen |
| **DWARF JUNIPER** | | | |
| (*Juniperus communis* 'Compressa') | 60cm (2ft) | | Evergreen |
| **HEBE** | | | |
| (*Hebe* 'Carl Teschner') | 30cm (12in) | Violet | Summer |
| **IVY (Small-leaved)** | | | |
| (*Hedera helix*) | Trailing to 60cm (2ft) | | Evergreen |
| **LAVENDER** | | | |
| (*Lavandula angustifolia* 'Hidcote') | 30-60cm (12-24in) | Purple, blue | Summer |
| **WINTER HEATHER** | | | |
| (*Erica carnea* 'Springwood White') | 15-30cm (6-12in) | White, pink | Winter |

*Top to bottom: periwinkle; pansy and campanula*

## *practical*
## project
## 2

### CONTROLLING
### CONTAINER
### GARDEN PESTS

Pests can be troublesome at any time of the year, but in early summer it seems sometimes that the entire greenfly population has descended on to your patch. Personally, I prefer not to use chemicals in the garden and, apart from the occasional infestation (which is invariably short-lived) container plants are not particularly troubled by pests. For one thing, pots are raised off the ground on feet or bricks, which deters all but the most athletic of slugs. I work on the principle that prevention is better than cure. Unhealthy plants which are struggling for survival in poor soil always seem to suffer. So it follows that healthy plants in generous-sized pots filled with sterilised compost should be able to withstand most attacks from pests. The following tasks should become part of any sensible container gardener's routine.

■ Keep the patio, balcony or other outside space clear of fallen leaves and debris. Regular sweeping under and around the pots will remove the habitat which slugs and snails need to survive.

■ Always use proprietary potting compost and repot plants regularly, rather than wait until they show signs of stress. In spring and summer, water and feed regularly to promote strong growth.

■ Encourage birds to visit the area by providing fresh water in summer and food in winter. Birds are excellent predators – they will eat caterpillars, slugs and aphids in summer and pick off the eggs or larvae in winter.

If these preventative measures are not enough, the chart opposite should help you to control any persistent pests using organic methods.

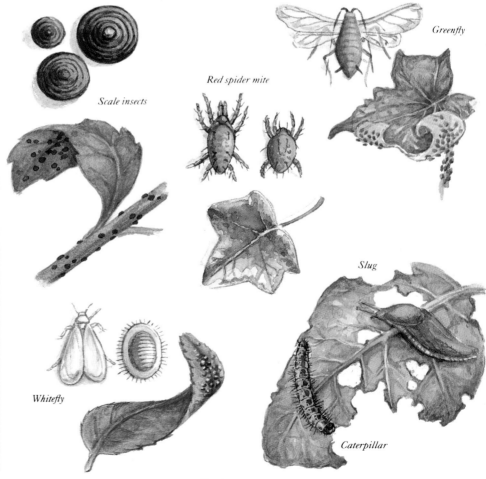

*Scale insects*

*Red spider mite*

*Greenfly*

*Slug*

*Whitefly*

*Caterpillar*

*Not drawn to scale*

## ORGANIC PEST CONTROL

| Pest | Damage caused | Manual method | Organic method | Wildlife controls |
|------|---------------|---------------|----------------|-------------------|
| **APHIDS** | | | | |
| Aphids, including blackfly and greenfly, are the most common garden pest | The sap is sucked from young leaves and stems, causing the plant to weaken | Pick off affected leaves and shoots. Knock off the aphids with a jet of water | Sprays made from soap or derris (although the latter kills ladybirds) | Blue-tits, ladybirds and hoverflies |
| **CATERPILLARS** | | | | |
| Caterpillars of moths and butterflies, particularly cabbage moths and whites | Leaves of young plants may be stripped completely | Check plants weekly and pick off caterpillars and eggs | Spray or dust with derris or pyrethrum (both are harmful to fish), but reapply regularly | Birds |
| **CUTWORM** | | | | |
| Moth caterpillars which live in the soil | Stems and roots underground are attacked. Caterpillars emerge at night to feed on new foliage | If noticed, pick off by hand. Repot plant in fresh compost | Not appropriate | Birds, particularly blackbirds which feed at ground level |
| **FROG HOPPERS** | | | | |
| Small green bugs that jump when disturbed | Blobs of white frothy 'spit' contain the nymph; damage is minimal | Knock off unsightly blobs by hand or with a jet of water | Not appropriate | No specific predators |
| **RED SPIDER MITE** | | | | |
| A pest of indoor and outdoor plants in hot summers | Leaves become discoloured and brittle | Cut off affected leaves. Clear up fallen leaves thoroughly in the autumn | Spray with insecticidal soap (which can kill ladybirds) | No specific predators |
| **SCALE INSECTS** | | | | |
| Small insects with a hard outer shell | Attacks fruit trees and ornamental shrubs and trees | Wipe trunk and branches with a damp sponge or cloth to dislodge | Not appropriate | Parasitic wasps |
| **SLUGS** | | | | |
| The most visible garden pests but they are easily controlled. Eggs are found in the soil | Large holes eaten out of leaves | Raise pots off ground and protect young growth with cloches. Keep area free of debris | Not appropriate | Birds, particularly ground-feeders; hedgehogs; frogs and toads |
| **WHITEFLY** | | | | |
| Tiny white flies that fly up in a cloud when disturbed | Looks worse than it is. A sticky residue on undersides of leaves which is covered by a harmless black mould | Pick off affected leaves. Hose down plants to remove residue | Spray with insecticidal soap (not safe for ladybirds) | No special predators |

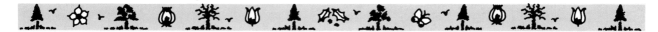

# JULY

The height of summer is the time to sit back, relax and enjoy the
good weather which, with luck, will last throughout the month. As
long as the plants get a regular soaking, the container garden
should be looking its best. The cool foliage of hostas and ferns
makes a perfect backdrop for the hot splashes of colour provided
by day lilies (Hemerocallis) and the true lilies, which are just
starting to show. For scent, Jasminum officinale takes over from
the honeysuckle, which is fading fast. Mophead and lacecap
hydrangeas have reached their prime and are almost perfect
container subjects, with long-lasting flowers and mottled foliage.
It is advisable to move hydrangea pots out of the fierce midday
sun – they will keep their fresh looks far better in dappled shade.
The gardener could be forgiven for being lazy this month and
doing very little, but those who like to exercise their creativity will
be thinking ahead to autumn. This is the time to put in autumn-
flowering bulbs like Colchicum and to order spring bulbs. It
might be hard to contemplate next year's show when this year is
only halfway through, but the bulb catalogues get more colourful
and enticing every year and make good holiday reading.
Don't neglect the weeds that somehow find their way into even
freshly planted pots. Weed seedlings will rob the main plant of
water and nutrients, which it can ill afford to give up at this
stage. Pull them out by hand – in a confined space there is no need
to resort to weedkillers. Other than the regular rituals of watering
and feeding, the only plants that might need attention are
tomatoes, which are putting on growth at an alarming rate. Tie
the stems in to bamboo canes and pinch out the top growth to keep
them within their allotted space.

# tasks

### FOR THE

## *month*

## CHECKLIST

- Pot-layer clematis, wisteria and honeysuckle
- Prune wisteria, fruit trees and bushes
- Clip box
- Plant autumn-flowering bulbs
- Take semi-ripe cuttings
- Thin summer-flowering jasmine
- Routine tasks: dead-head flowers, control weeds, continue watering and feeding

### LAYERING CLIMBERS

Clematis, wisteria and honeysuckle can be layered at any time between now and autumn. Layering is a form of propagation which involves pinning down part of a flexible stem into the soil so that roots form at this point.

■ Prepare a pot with potting compost.

■ Untie a stem with leaf buds and pull it down, with the pot positioned so that the stem can be anchored easily.

■ Wound the underpart of the stem at the point where it lies on the soil surface by scraping off a little of the outer bark.

■ Peg the stem down securely into the soil with wire or a stone.

■ Once rooted, sever the stem from the parent plant and grow on, increasing the pot size when necessary.

### PRUNING WISTERIA

Established wisterias should have side shoots pruned back to within 15cm (6in) of the main stem. The whippy young growths of newer plants should be reduced by half their length.

### PRUNING FRUIT

Small bush apples grown in pots should be pruned now to remove any crossing or overcrowded branches. The aim is to keep an open framework of branches growing outwards. Vigorously growing fig trees can be thinned by the removal of overcrowded shoots. Carry out summer pruning of espalier apple and pear trees as shown, cutting back side shoots (laterals) to leave three to five leaves on each shoot.

### CLIPPING BOX

Box and other hedging plants grown as shaped specimens should be clipped to shape this month. Fast-growing plants such as *Lonicera nitida* or privet will need to be clipped again next month.

### NOTE

■ *Remove weeds regularly to prevent them competing with plants for food and moisture* ■

### PLANTING AUTUMN-FLOWERING BULBS

Autumn-flowering bulbs provide colour at a time when other flowers may be past their best. Colchicums, autumn-flowering crocus and sternbergias will be available now and can be planted among shrubs growing in large containers.

*Cyclamen hederifolium* flowers between late summer and late autumn and is well suited to growing in the light shade of shrubs, where the attractively marbled foliage will continue to provide interest in spring and summer. Make holes 5cm (2in) deep and plant in small clusters so that the bulbs are not touching each other. Cover with soil and insert a plant tag with the name as a reminder not to disturb the soil.

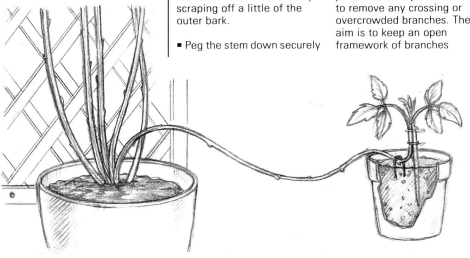

## TAKING SEMI-RIPE CUTTINGS

Between now and next month stem cuttings of many shrubs can be taken. Cuttings taken at this time of year are from semi-ripe wood and should root easily. They can be overwintered outside in a cold frame or in a frost-free place, and repotted in spring.

■ Choose non-flowering shoots and take cuttings 7.5-15cm (3-6in) long.

■ Trim the base and remove the lower leaves so that none will touch the soil when planted.

■ Fill pots with a proprietary seed and cuttings compost and insert three or four cuttings to a pot, around the edge.

■ Cover the whole pot loosely with a plastic bag supported on a wire hoop (a simple hoop can be made from coathanger wire), or place in an unheated propagator until the plants have rooted.

## THINNING SUMMER JASMINE

Summer jasmine can be thinned if plants are taking up too much room. Shortening stems will only encourage bushiness; instead, take out the entire length of dead or overcrowded stems to ground level.

## DEAD-HEADING FLOWERS

To keep containers looking good, dead-head faded flowers regularly. This will also encourage annual bedding plants to carry on flowering throughout the season rather than setting seed.

## SHRUBS FOR SEMI-RIPE CUTTINGS

*Camellia japonica*
*Ceanothus × burkwoodii*
*Daphne mezereum*
*Hebe*
*Hibiscus (Hibiscus syriacus)*
*Hydrangea macrophylla*
*Lavender*
*Lilac (Syringa microphylla)*
*Rhododendron*
*Santolina*
*Viburnum tinus*
*Weigela florida*

*HELP WITH ROOTING*
*Hormone rooting powders are used to help induce root formation on cuttings and can increase the success rate. Tip a small amount of powder on to an old lid, and dip the cut end in. Knock the cutting gently to get rid of excess powder and insert in the compost.*

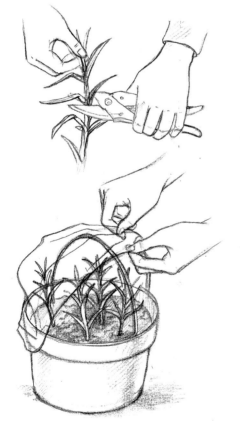

*JULY*

# plants

## OF THE

## *month*

## *1*

### CAMPANULA
#### (*Campanula carpatica*)

This is a useful spreading plant for large troughs or sinks where it can tumble over the edge, forming a carpet of summer colour. Campanula is easy to care for and can be left in position for several years.

| | |
|---|---|
| type | Perennial |
| flowers | Blue, purple or white; mid- to late summer |
| height | 23-30cm (9-12in) |
| spread | 30-38cm (12-15in) |
| planting | Autumn or spring |
| site | Sun or partial shade; in troughs, sinks or pots |
| compost | Well-drained, multi-purpose |
| care | Snip off flowers as they fade. Divide and replant every three years in spring |
| propagation | By division in spring |
| varieties | 'Blue Moonlight' is pale blue; 'Bressingham White' is white; 'Dickson's Gold' has bright gold foliage and pale lilac flowers |

###  COMMON WHITE JASMINE
#### (*Jasminum officinale*)

This vigorous, hardy climber needs a large tub, but it is excellent for growing against walls or fences or for twining around arches and pergolas. The stems need to be tied in to a firm support such as a trellis, as they will not climb unaided. The flowers are sweetly scented and will last right through to autumn – an ideal plant for an outdoor patio or eating area.

| | |
|---|---|
| type | Deciduous climber |
| flowers | White, fragrant; summer to mid-autumn |
| height | To 10m (30ft) |
| spread | To 6m (18ft) |
| planting | Autumn or spring |
| site | Sun or light shade; in large tubs or barrels |
| compost | Loam-based |
| care | Water well in dry periods. Use a liquid feed monthly from late spring to early autumn. Take out any crowded stems at ground level, in midsummer |
| propagation | By semi-ripe cuttings in late summer |
| varieties | 'Aureo-variegatum' has yellow, variegated leaves |
| related species | *Jasminum polyanthum* is usually |

grown as a conservatory plant, but may survive outdoors in areas with mild winters. It grows to a more compact 3m (10ft) and has fragrant, pale pink flowers which appear from spring to early summer

### HYDRANGEA
#### (*Hydrangea macrophylla*)

This rounded shrub with its lacy blue or pink flowers grows well in a large pot or tub and is very easy to care for. The flowerheads are very variable, changing from blue to pink according to the growing medium, and this is part of their charm. If you want to retain the blue colour, you need to use an ericaceous (acid) compost. Even the faded blooms are an attractive buff colour and can be used in dried flower arrangements.

| | |
|---|---|
| type | Deciduous shrub |
| flowers | Pink, blue, white; midsummer to early autumn |
| height | 1.2-2m (4-6ft) |
| spread | 1.2-2m (4-6ft) |
| planting | Autumn or spring |
| site | Sheltered, lightly shaded position; avoid positions where growth can be damaged by early morning sun after frost |
| compost | Loam based or multi-purpose. To retain blue colouring, use an ericaceous (lime-free) compost |
| care | Mulch the surface of the compost in spring with well-rotted manure, home-made compost or specially bought mulch mix. Keep the soil moist, but not waterlogged, in summer |
| propagation | By semi-ripe cuttings in late summer |
| varieties | Hydrangeas are divided into two groups: mopheads, with tight, rounded flowerheads, and lacecaps, with flatter, lacier flowers<br>**Mopheads:** 'Generale Vicomtesse de Vibraye' is sky blue or pink; 'Deutschland' is deep rose pink or mid-blue<br>**Lacecaps:** 'Lanarth White' has white outer florets with pink or blue centres; 'Tricolor' has variegated foliage with pink or blue flowers |
| related species | The climbing hydrangea (*H. petiolaris*) can be grown in a large tub against a shady wall, |

where it will attach itself with no support using aerial roots. The creamy-white flowers are not as showy as the mopheads or lacecaps, but it is well worth growing in a spot which doesn't get a lot of sun and where other climbers would fail

## DAY LILY
### *(Hemerocallis* hybrids)

Most of the day lilies for sale in garden centres are hybrids of the original Japanese species. All are hardy perennials which, once established, are trouble free. The flowers are large and showy, trumpet-shaped blooms in shades of yellow, pink and red, and the strap-shaped leaves form bold clumps of foliage.

| | |
|---|---|
| **type** | Herbaceous perennial |
| **flowers** | Red, yellow, pink, orange; summer |
| **height** | 60-90cm (2-3ft) |
| **spread** | 60cm (2ft) |
| **planting** | Autumn or spring, 60cm (2ft) apart in large tubs, or singly in individual pots |
| **site** | Sun or light shade; tubs or pots |
| **compost** | Multi-purpose |
| **care** | Water freely during long, dry spells. After flowering, cut the stems down almost to ground level. Day lilies prefer not to be disturbed, so replace the top 5cm (2in) of compost each spring rather than repot. Only divide when the clumps become so congested that they stop flowering |
| **propagation** | Lift and divide clumps (see Care) in autumn or spring |
| **varieties** | 'Bonanza' is light orange with a maroon centre; 'Stafford' has deep red flowers with yellow throats. Dwarf varieties (under 60cm/2ft) are also available from specialist nurseries |

# *practical* project

## PLANTING A HERB/ STRAWBERRY POT

The urn-shaped terracotta pots with lots of planting holes in the sides are known as 'strawberry pots', although their use is by no means limited to growing strawberries. The smaller ones are sometimes called 'parsley pots', but in fact they can be used for growing a whole range of herbs. Any plants that are naturally compact or have a slightly trailing habit are suitable for growing in a strawberry pot, including alpines, miniature bulbs, herbs and, of course, strawberries. They are an excellent way of growing a greater number of plants than would be possible in conventional pots, particularly where space is limited.

### HOW TO PLANT

■ Ensure that the pot has drainage holes, and cover with a layer of broken crocks. Add a layer of clay aggregate pebbles or stone chippings.

■ For pots over 60cm (2ft) high, add a central drainage column to ensure that water flows freely through the whole pot. Make a cylinder of fine-mesh chicken wire or garden netting, about 7.5-10cm (3-4in) in diameter and slightly shorter than the height of the pot. Insert the cylinder in the centre of the pot and fill with pebbles or chippings.

■ Fill the pot with compost, up to the level of the lowest planting openings. For strawberries, use a loam-based potting compost; for alpines and herbs, mix the compost with grit to prevent it becoming waterlogged (see p20).

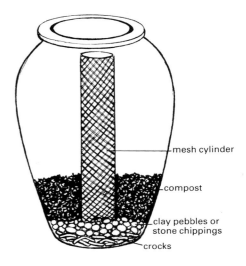

— mesh cylinder

— compost

— clay pebbles or stone chippings

— crocks

■ Push in the plants, roots first, through the lower openings. Cover the roots with more potting compost and firm down. Insert plants into all the lower openings before filling with compost up to the next layer.

■ When all the plants are in place, plant up the top surface of the pot, taking care not to clog up the drainage cylinder with compost. Water carefully at first, so as not to wash the compost out through the openings.

### AFTERCARE

■ Water frequently in hot, dry weather.

■ Apply a weekly liquid feed to strawberries as soon as the fruits have begun to appear. Herbs and other plants will only need feeding once every two weeks.

■ Alternatively, use slow-release fertiliser spikes or pellets.

■ Turn the pot once a week, to ensure that all the planting pockets receive the same amount of sunlight.

■ Harvest strawberries in mid- to late summer (alpine strawberries may fruit into the autumn). Trim off any dead or yellowing leaves. Herbs can be snipped off as needed through the season.

■ In autumn, remove any annual herbs such as basil and parsley and cut back perennials like thyme, oregano and sage. Strawberry plants should be discarded every two to three years and planted again in the spring.

### RENEWING A HERB POT

Pots planted permanently with herbs can be renewed to prevent them looking straggly and uncared for. This is best done in spring or early autumn, *not* in the heat of summer.

■ Remove the plants from the top of the pot

### RING THE CHANGES

*If you want to use a strawberry pot in a less conventional manner, plant it up for winter interest. Put one or two ferns in the top of the compost – these are shallow rooting and will do very well in this kind of pot. The planting pockets can be filled with species crocus such as the yellow* Crocus chrysanthus *or the white* C. biflorus. *Both flower in late winter and neither will grow above 7.5cm (3in) high. As an alternative to the ferns, plant a slow-growing dwarf conifer such as* Chamaecyparis lawsoniana *'Ellwoods Pillar', which will look good all year round (see p67 for a list).*

with a trowel. Dig out the compost layer by layer, carefully removing all the plants.

■ Discard any that are too old and leggy. Those which have simply outgrown their planting pockets should be divided to produce more plants.

■ If necessary, add more pebbles or stone chippings to the bottom of the pot.

■ Fill with compost up to the bottom layer of holes and replace any original plants which are still healthy. Add new or divided plants to fill the gaps.

■ Pack the compost well about their roots before filling up to the next layer.

### PLANTING IDEAS

**ALL PARSLEY**
**suitable for smaller sizes of planter**

**MIXED HERBS**
**Sage – *Salvia officinalis*** (green) or **'Tricolour'** (pink and cream)
**Thyme – *Thymus* × *citriodorus*** **'Silver Queen'** (variegated, lemon-scented leaves); **'Aureus'** (golden leaves)
**Oregano – *Oreganum vulgare*** **'Compactum'** (compact form)

**ALPINES AND SUCCULENTS**
***Arabis ferdinandii-coburgii*** (white flowers)
***Armeria juniperina*** (pink flowers)
***Campanula arvatica*** (dwarf, trailing, blue flowers)
***Echeveria glauca*** (rosettes of blue-grey leaves)
***Sempervivum arachnoideum*** (cobweb house-leek, leaf tips spun together with white strands)

**STRAWBERRIES**
**'Baron Solemacher'** (alpine variety, ripens in late summer and autumn)
**'Cambridge Favourite'** (midsummer variety)

**TRAILING SUMMER PLANTS**
**Campanula**
**Ivy-leaved pelargonium**
**Lobelia**
**Nasturtium**

*MINT MENACE*
*It is best to avoid mints, which will soon swamp the other plants in the herb pot and quickly become leggy and unsightly. They are best grown in a conventional container on their own.*

# plants
## OF THE
## *month*
## *2*

## HOSTA
### *(Hosta species and varieties)*

One of the best foliage plants for container growing, the hosta is a favourite of town gardeners, who use it to fill all the shady areas where little else will grow. Hostas may be popular, but they are certainly not ordinary, with a wide range of variation in leaf colour, texture and form. The flowers, though short-lived, are in pretty shades of lilac and mauve. The great thing about growing hostas in pots is that they are out of the way of slugs – probably the plant's worst enemy in a conventional garden.

| | |
|---|---|
| type | Herbaceous perennial |
| flowers | Lilac, mauve, purple, white; produced on stalks above the leaves in mid- to late summer |
| height | 60-90cm (2-3ft) |
| spread | 60cm (2ft) |
| planting | Autumn or spring |
| site | Light shade, will tolerate deep shade; in large, individual pots |
| compost | Moist, loam-based |
| care | Keep compost moist, particularly during dry spells. Mulch the surface of the compost in spring with well-rotted manure, peat substitute, leaf mould or specially bought mulch mix. Leave undisturbed until division is necessary – every three or four years |

| | |
|---|---|
| propagation | Lift and divide plants in early spring and replant the crowns immediately |
| recommended species | *H. albo-marginata* – height and spread 45cm (18in); small, narrow leaves with white margins, lilac flowers<br>*H. crispula* – height and spread 60cm (2ft); ribbed leaves with prominent white margins, lilac-purple flowers<br>*H. fortunei* – height and spread 60-90cm (2-3ft); oval, grey-green leaves, lilac flowers. The young leaves of 'Albopicta' are pale green, almost yellow, turning darker as the plant matures<br>*H. sieboldiana* – height and spread 60cm (2ft); glossy, strongly veined leaves, off-white flowers. 'Bressingham Blue' has blue-green leaves |

## SNAPDRAGON
### *(Antirrhinum majus)*

This is one of the most popular of all summer flowers – and rightly so. The fragrant flower spikes appear in midsummer and continue flowering until the first frosts. They are a great favourite with children, who soon discover how they got their name – squeezing the flowers makes the jaws open like a dragon, and snap shut again to capture unsuspecting insects. Garden varieties are available in every conceivable colour, from tall varieties reaching 1m (3ft) to the dwarf forms suitable for windowboxes.

| | |
|---|---|
| type | Half-hardy annual |
| flowers | White, yellow, pink, orange, red; midsummer to autumn |
| height | Tall: 60-90cm (2-3ft); intermediate 38-60cm (15-24in); low-growing: 23-39cm (9-15in); dwarf: 10-23cm (4-9in) |
| spread | 15-38cm (6-15in) |
| planting | Set out bedding plants in late spring or early summer |
| site | Sunny; pots and windowboxes |
| compost | Multi-purpose |
| care | Snip off flowerheads to prolong flowering. Liquid feed every two weeks during flowering. Water regularly, especially windowboxes and small pots which dry out quickly. Discard plants in early autumn |
| propagation | From seed sown in early spring |

recommended   *Intermediate:*
varieties    'Cinderella Mixed' – mixed colours
             'Monarch' – single colours

             *Low-growing:*
             'F Sweetheart' – mixed colours

             *Dwarf:*
             'Magic Carpet Mixed' – mixed
             colours
             'Little Gem Mixed' – mixed colours
             'Tom Thumb Mixed' – mixed
             colours

## FRENCH MARIGOLD
### (*Tagetes patula*)

This cheerful summer-flowering marigold originates not from France, but from Mexico. Its compact shape, vibrant colour range and long flowering season make it one of the mainstays of summer container planting. Although not difficult to raise from seed, marigolds are most widely available as bedding plants in late spring. They can then be put straight into pots of compost and out on to the patio or balcony for an instant display.

type        Half-hardy annual
flowers     Yellow, deep orange, red and
            brown; early summer to early
            autumn
height      30cm (12in)
spread      30cm (12in)
planting    As bedding plants from late
            spring to late summer
site        In full sun; hanging baskets,
            window boxes, pots
compost     Multi-purpose
care        Water frequently in dry weather.
            Snip off flowerheads as they fade.
            Feed fortnightly with a liquid
            fertiliser. Discard plants at the
            end of the growing season
propagation Sow seeds indoors in early spring
            and plant out in late spring or early
            summer when the danger of frosts
            has passed
varieties   Single and double blooms
            available: 'Cinnabar' is a single
            deep red with a yellow centre,
            'Sunny' is a single golden yellow.
            Several mixed colour varieties are
            also available
related     *T. signata pumila* is a dwarf
species     compact form, reaching no more
            than 23cm (9in), making it an ideal
            choice for window boxes. The

flowers are smaller but borne in great profusion. 'Tangerine Gem' is a deep orange, 'Lemon Gem' is lemon yellow

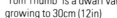

## NASTURTIUM
### (*Tropaeolum majus*)

Nasturtiums are among the most versatile of annual flowers, whether they are cascading from a hanging basket, trailing from a window box or allowed to scramble up a trellis. Quick growing and easy to care for, they provide instant colour and attractive foliage.

type        Hardy annual
flowers     Yellow, orange, red; summer
height      To 2.5m (8ft)
spread      60cm (2ft)
planting    As bedding plants in late spring
site        Full sun; in tubs, hanging baskets,
            window boxes
compost     Multi-purpose
care        Water frequently in hot weather.
            Use a liquid feed every fortnight
            throughout the growing season
propagation Sow seeds outdoors in mid-spring
            and plant into permanent positions
            in late spring or early summer
varieties   'Tom Thumb' is a dwarf variety
            growing to 30cm (12in)

# AUGUST

*All the world seems to be winding down this month – and that includes the container gardener. Lazy summer days should be savoured to the full; this period of inactivity is all too short. The one task that cannot be neglected is regular watering to prevent pots, windowboxes and hanging baskets from drying out: containers planted in late spring are often left to fend for themselves through the relentless heat of summer. Keep up the daily watering routine and snip off flowerheads as they fade. A fortnightly liquid feed will keep most annuals and bedding plants going right into autumn.*

*Keeping plants fresh while you are away on holiday is always a problem. Self-watering containers are one answer, well-trained neighbours another. Makeshift bucket-and-wick watering systems are fine for most containers, and there will be no-one around to see them, no matter how bizarre they look.*

*In most regions it is a little early for planting spring bulbs, but it is a good time to propagate your favourite shrubs from cuttings. If you don't have the space or the inclination for propagation, you will just have to mark time until the new season of shrubs starts in garden centres in early autumn. In the meantime, be content with the current, late summer show. The theme of powdery blues and mauves seem to suit the langorous, tail end of summer; lavenders, salvias, heathers and hebes are all flowering generously.*

# tasks

## FOR THE

## *month*

## CHECKLIST

- Tidy and trim perennials and clip shrubs
- Collect seeds
- Set up system for holiday watering
- Order new trees, shrubs, roses and fruit
- Continue taking cuttings
- Routine tasks: dead-heading, watering, feeding, weeding
- Check camellias

### TIDYING UP

Clump-forming perennials like hardy geraniums and campanula can look rather untidy after they have finished flowering. Remove flower stalks and tidy away general plant debris. Apart from keeping containers looking fresh, regular clearing up helps to deter soil pests and prevent the spread of disease.

### TRIMMING AND CLIPPING

The time for clipping lavender to shape is early spring, but bushes can be kept looking decorative if the flower stalks are removed as they fade and dry.

Clipped specimens of strong-growing privet and *Lonicera nitida* may need to be trimmed again if they are looking untidy.

Shaped bay trees can also be given a light trim, and the longer clippings used for cuttings (see p73).

### COLLECTING SEEDS

The seeds of many flowering plants can be collected now and saved for sowing in the spring.

■ When ripe, snip off complete seedheads and place them upside down in an open paper bag.

■ Hold the bag closed and shake gently to dislodge the seeds from their capsules.

■ Spread out the contents on a tray and separate the seeds from any debris.

■ Pour them into airtight containers (such as glass herb jars), label and store in a cool, dark place.

### HOLIDAY WATERING

Leaving a garden at the hottest time of year can be a problem, and container plants are more at risk from drying out than those growing in the ground. If pots cannot be watered and the garden has to remain untended for more than a few days, take as many precautions as possible to guard against water loss.

■ Immediately before you go, water plants thoroughly.

■ Move the most vulnerable plants into the shade, and add a layer of mulch mix or stone chippings.

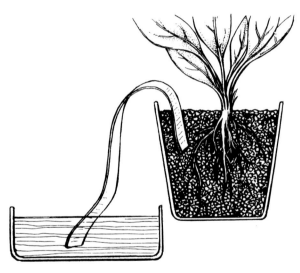

## MOBILE CONTAINERS

*For a practical way of moving large pots around the patio, take a wooden board or old tray slightly larger than the base of the pot, and screw a set of furniture castors into the base. Purpose-built slatted wood plant 'trolleys' are also available.*

### REVITALISING CAMELLIAS

It is easy to forget the long-suffering, evergreen camellias at this time of the year, when there are so many other, more colourful plants in the garden. However, a little care now will ensure that they are in good shape for winter and spring when their colourful blooms are so welcome. The roots should always be kept cool, so move the pots to a shady position. Water thoroughly and apply a 5cm (2in) mulch of well-rotted manure, leaf-mould or ericaceous compost. This will ensure that the compost does not dry out and will help to keep the roots cool. As the autumn rains arrive, the nutrients will be washed down into the compost. Give the leaves a wipe with a damp cloth to remove summer dust and bring back their glossy shine.

**FRUIT FOR CONTAINERS**
*(See Appendix 1 for details on growing fruit in containers)*

**Apples**
**Fig**
**Grape vine**
**Dwarf peach**
**Dwarf nectarine**

**Peaches, figs and nectarines need a position in full sun in order to fruit well**

- If possible, plunge small pots into larger containers of damp compost.

- For short periods of time small pots, which are most likely to dry out quickly, can be rested on trays of moistened water-retentive pebbles.

- For longer absences, place pots in trays lined with capillary matting. Arrange the matting so that one end is resting in a partly filled sink or bowl of water.

- Larger pots that are difficult to move can be kept moist using special wicks made from capillary matting or towelling. Push one end of the wick into the compost and drape the other into a bucket filled with water.

### NOTE

- *For precious collections of plants and long holidays, it is well worth investing in a micro-irrigation kit with an electronic timer (see p61)* ■

# plants
## OF THE
## *month*

## AFRICAN LILY
### *(Agapanthus* 'Headbourne Hybrids'*)*

Many people think that agapanthus are not hardy enough to be grown outdoors, but the garden hybrids will survive most winters, particularly if grown up against a sheltered wall. They make handsome container plants, with their tall, stately stems, strap-like leaves and startling blue flowers.

| | |
|---|---|
| type | Fleshy-rooted perennial |
| flowers | Shades of blue; midsummer to early autumn |
| height | 75cm (30in) |
| spread | 38-45cm (15-18in) |
| planting | Mid-spring; set the crowns 5cm (2in) deep and do not disturb after planting |
| site | Sunny, sheltered position; in large pots and tubs, preferably at the foot of a warm wall |
| compost | Multi-purpose |
| care | Water well until established and in dry spells. Cut stems to ground level after flowering. In late autumn, protect crowns against frost with a thick mulch of coarse sand |
| propagation | By division in spring |

*Heather 'Golden Haze'*

## HEATHER
### *(Calluna vulgaris)*

The garden forms of *Calluna vulgaris* are descendants of the true wild heather seen growing on moorlands and hillsides at this time of year. They are easy to grow in pots, where they can be given the lime-free growing medium they prefer. Heathers start flowering in mid- to late summer and often last until the end of autumn. There is also a winter-flowering species *(Erica carnea)* which can be grown outdoors in containers.

| | |
|---|---|
| type | Evergreen shrub |
| flowers | Purple, pink, white; late summer to autumn |
| height | 30-45cm (12-18in) |
| spread | 30-45cm (12-18in) |
| planting | Autumn or spring; put the plants in deeply so that the foliage rests on the compost |
| site | Sunny, away from overhanging trees or shrubs; in pots or troughs on balconies, patios and roof gardens |
| compost | Ericaceous (lime-free) |
| care | Water well until plants are established, then water in spring and during dry spells in summer. Apply a layer of mulch (peat or peat substitute) in spring. Leave the decorative dry flowerheads on the plant through the winter; clip over with shears in spring |
| propagation | By semi-ripe cuttings in late summer |
| varieties | 'Gold Haze' – golden foliage and white flowers; 'H.E. Beale' – double pink flowers; 'Silver Queen' – dwarf (15cm/6in) with silver-grey foliage and purple flowers; 'Sunset' – golden leaves in summer, bronze in winter |

## LAVENDER
### *(Lavandula angustifolia)*

This Mediterranean shrub makes a good container plant, being compact and resilient to drought. The characteristic fragrance comes from the flowers, as well as from the silvery-grey leaves, which are strongly aromatic. A good shrub for a patio seating area.

| | |
|---|---|
| type | Evergreen shrub |
| flowers | Purple or blue flower spikes; midsummer to early autumn |

| | |
|---|---|
| height | 1-1.2m (3-4ft) |
| spread | 1m (3ft) |
| planting | Autumn or spring |
| site | Sunny; in pots on patios, balconies, roof gardens |
| compost | Well-drained, multi-purpose |
| care | Trim off fading flowerheads in late summer. Cut back to just above the old wood in early spring if the plant is looking straggly. When the bush gets too woody, discard and replace with new plants |
| propagation | By semi-ripe cuttings in late summer |
| varieties | 'Hidcote' is a more compact 60cm (2ft) with deep purple-blue flowers; 'Nana Alba' is a dwarf white form with silvery-green foliage (height and spread 30cm/12in) |

### SALVIA
#### (*Salvia farinacea*)

The understated blues and purples of salvia make a welcome change from the vivid colours of early summer. Clumps of salvia, grown in terracotta pots amongst lavender, rosemary and purple sage (also from the salvia family) give the container garden a co-ordinated, uncluttered look. Salvia is easy to grow from seed, or buy young plants in early summer.

| | |
|---|---|
| type | Half-hardy annual |
| flowers | Purple, blue, white; midsummer to mid-autumn |

| | |
|---|---|
| height | 60cm (2ft) |
| spread | 30cm (1ft) |
| planting | Early summer, 30cm (12in) apart |
| site | Sunny; in pots on patios and balconies |
| compost | Well-drained, multi-purpose |
| care | Pinch out the growing tips of young plants to encourage side shoots. Discard plants in autumn |
| propagation | Sow seed under cover in early spring |
| varieties | 'Victoria' is a deep, violet blue; 'White Victory' has silvery-white flower spikes |
| garden hybrid | *Salvia × superba* forms a dense clump of purple-blue flowers (60 × 60cm/2ft × 2ft) |

### ESCALLONIA
#### (*Escallonia* var.)

The fact that this evergreen shrub is considered tender in some areas is all the more reason to grow it as a container plant that can be moved under cover when frost threatens. The glossy evergreen leaves will stand much buffeting from salt spray and sea water, which makes it a popular plant in coastal gardens. The flowers are rather like apple-blossom, in shades ranging from white to the deepest rose-pink, and appear continuously throughout the summer.

| | |
|---|---|
| type | Evergreen shrub (tender in some areas) |
| flowers | White, pink; early summer to mid-autumn |
| height | 2m (6ft) |
| spread | 1.5m (5ft) |
| planting | Plant in mid-autumn or mid-spring |
| site | In full sun; against a south-facing wall if possible; in tubs, and half-barrels |
| compost | Loam-based |
| care | Remove flowering growths after flowering. No other pruning required. Water regularly in dry spells and use a liquid feed once a month in spring and summer |
| propagation | From semi-ripe cuttings in late summer |
| varieties | 'C.F. Ball' is considered the hardiest variety; it bears red flowers from early summer onwards. 'Apple Blossom' is a compact 1.5 × 1.5m (5 × 5ft) and has white flowers with a pink tinge. 'Glory of Donard' is a deep rose-pink |

# *practical* project

## PLANTING AND FIXING WALL POTS

### POTS FOR SCENT

Combine lemon-scented thyme (*Thymus × citriodorus*) with dwarf nicotiana (*Nicotiana* 'Domino F1') in lime-green or white, for a fragrant summer display.

Larger baskets and mangers could hold one of the scented geraniums such as *Pelargonium* 'Tomentosum' which has a strong peppermint scent. Dwarf *Pelargonium* 'Little Gem' smells of roses and is suitable for the smallest wall pot.

By using the walls around the house and patio we can significantly extend the amount of planting space available. Wall planters are ideal for balconies, basements and patios, adding much-needed greenery to bare expanses of brick or stone. Not only are they decorative features but the plants in them should grow well, particularly on sunny walls which will reflect a lot of warmth.

The one drawback with wall pots is that they are usually too sheltered to receive a reasonable amount of rainfall. Also, most of these pots have a small planting capacity, which means that regular watering (twice daily in high summer) is vital if the plants are not to shrivel up and die. This can be difficult if the pots are sited high up on a wall: try to position them below a window, where they can be topped up from above.

Remember, if you are leaning out of windows or using ladders to water the pots, always put safety considerations first. Make sure that the drips from newly watered pots don't fall on people or patio furniture; ideally, wall pots should be fitted with integral drip trays, but many are not.

One way around the size problem is to use the wrought-iron 'mangers' which are appearing in garden centres. Mangers tend to be larger than conventional wall pots and will need to be lined with black polythene and moss.

### DISPLAYING WALL POTS

■ Staggered groups of odd numbers (three or five) look better than single isolated pots.

■ Symmetrical arrangements can work along an expanse of wall or fence, where the pots are sited at regular intervals – for example, on every fence post – keeping the height level all the way along.

### PLANTING A WALL POT

■ Plant the pot before fixing it to the wall.

■ Cover the base with a 2.5cm (1in) layer of gravel or small stone chippings for drainage.

■ Add a 5cm (2in) layer of potting compost.

■ Plant any bulbs or upright plants towards the back and centre, and plant trailers at the front, where they can tumble down freely.

■ Fill in any gaps with compost and firm down well. Water thoroughly and allow to drain. Add more compost if necessary to bring the level up to 2.5cm (1in) below the rim.

■ Always detach the pot from the wall before attempting to remove or repot plants.

*WALL BASKETS*
*Wire baskets should be lined with moss or black polythene (punctured with drainage holes) and planted in the same way as other wall pots. Trailing plants can also be pushed in around the sides of the basket.*

# *practical*
# project

## PLANTING AND
## FIXING WALL POTS

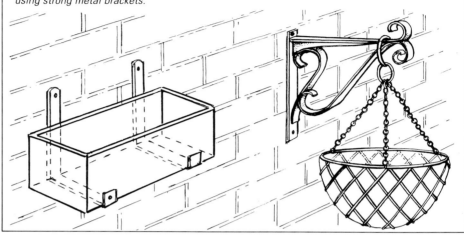

### DON'T FORGET

*Conventional windowboxes (see p65) and hanging baskets (p54) can be attached to the wall using strong metal brackets.*

### FIXING WALL POTS

Terracotta and stone wall pots generally have one or two keyhole-shaped openings in the back plate to allow the pot to be wall-mounted easily. On brick walls, drill a hole using a masonry drill, tap in a rawlplug and insert a large-headed screw. Leave the head protruding by about 1cm (½in) to allow the opening to slip over it. Some pots come with their own brackets, plates and screws, and corresponding instructions for fixing.

### PLANTS FOR WALL POTS

It is best to choose small or slow-growing species that won't outgrow their allotted space too quickly. Miniature bulbs are a good choice: for spring, try miniature daffodils such as *Narcissus tazetta* 'Minnow' or *Narcissus triandrus albus*; for a late winter show, use the purple-flowered dwarf *Iris reticulata*. Both can be planted in early autumn.

For trailing plants it is hard to beat the small-leaved ivies *(Hedera helix)*, which can be left in place all year round. For variegated leaves, 'Glacier' is a good variety with silver colouring, whilst 'Goldheart' is also variegated but with gold markings.

Campanulas, pansies *(Viola × wittrockiana* hybrids, summer- and winter–flowering) and drumstick primulas *(Primula denticulata)* will extend the colour range and still look in proportion with the dimensions of the pot. Larger wire baskets can include trailing pelargoniums or lobelias.

### Kitchen-window wall herbs

Try attaching pots within reach of the open window. This is a very convenient way to grow some of the frequently used herbs such as mint, parsley, chervil, basil and chives. The small pots are best removed in winter, then cleaned and replanted for the following summer. Miniature strawberry pots which have two or more planting pockets can be used for a small crop of alpine strawberries.

*Chervil*

*Chives*

# SEPTEMBER

As the calendar moves on into the first month of autumn, a wave of planning and planting can begin. This is also the harvest season: the time to gather in any produce grown in pots or windowboxes such as French and runner beans, tomatoes and apples. Don't be too keen to dismantle the annual flower displays in tubs and hanging baskets – continue to water and dead-head them to prolong their life until the end of the month. As the autumn equinox approaches and the days become noticeably shorter, natural growth is slowing down. This means that plants won't need as much sustenance and feeding can be reduced. Towards the end of the month frosts are a danger in many areas, and houseplants and tender plants spending the summer outdoors should be brought under cover. This releases space on the balcony or patio for a whole new range of planting, including bulbs, evergreens, conifers, heathers and winter perennials. Although the garden centres and catalogues are trying hard to lure container gardeners at this time of year, it can seem as if you are not getting a lot for your money. After all, a deciduous shrub, devoid of flowers and starting to shed its leaves, is hardly the most inviting prospect. Similarly, it takes a great leap of faith to dive into those garden centre 'bran tubs' piled high with brown, flaky bulbs. In this case, however, appearances are definitely deceptive. It is far better to plant shrubs in the autumn than wait until the flowers appear in spring or early summer, because you will have the benefit of watching the leaves unfurl and the buds appear. Likewise, with planning, it is possible to have bulbs appearing throughout winter and spring, starting with snowdrops and miniature irises in midwinter, followed by crocuses, early narcissi and a final splash of colour from the tulips.

# tasks
## FOR THE
## *month*

*IMPORTED PESTS*
*Before bringing in plants for the winter, check them for aphids, snails and soil pests and, once inside, continue checking occasionally.*

*BULB BONANZA*
*To make the most of space and prolong the flowering period, bulbs can be planted in layers in the same container. Plant earlier-flowering varieties on top, later-flowering varieties below. Take care not to place bulbs exactly over one another.*

**MINIATURE BULBS**
**TO PLANT**
***Chionodoxa, Crocus, Scilla***
PD = 7.5cm (3in)
***Iris histrioides* 'Major', *I. reticulata***
PD = 7.5cm (3in)
**Miniature narcissi 'Tête à Tête',**
'February Gold', 'Jack Snipe',
'Peeping Tom' PD = 15cm (6in)
***Muscari armeniacum,***
***M.botryoides*** PD = 7.5cm (3in)

**KEY**
PD = Planting depths

## CHECKLIST

- Bring in tender plants
- Plant spring-flowering bulbs
- Plant bulbs for indoor flowering
- Plant new evergreens and conifers
- Plant new climbers
- Plant perennials

### BRINGING IN TENDER PLANTS

Houseplants, cool conservatory plants, pelargoniums and tender fuchsias should be brought in before the first frosts. Pelargoniums and fuchsias do not need much heat over winter, so the best place to keep them is in an unheated porch or bedroom. If you have only limited space inside, just bring in one or two of the best plants from which to take cuttings next spring.

### NOTE

- *Hardy fuchsias like* F. magellanica *can remain unprotected in the garden over winter. Cut back hard in early spring as new shoots appear at the base of the plant (see p31)* ▪

### PLANTING BULBS

With the exception of tulips, planting of spring-flowering bulbs can begin now. Miniatures and dwarf varieties are best suited to small pots and windowboxes, and the foliage is less obtrusive when it dies back after flowering.

Bulbs that were lifted in late spring can now be replanted. Dispose of any that are soft or shrivelled.

Tulip and full-size daffodil bulbs can be planted to a

depth of 30cm (12in). In fact, where these bulbs are to remain part of the permanent planting scheme, it is best to plant deeply, so that later planting and lifting of summer bedding does not disturb them.

### NOTE

- *Tulips should not be planted until mid- to late autumn. Bulbs planted earlier are more susceptible to 'tulip fire' – a virus which attacks in early autumn* ▪

### BULBS FOR FORCING INDOORS

Bulbs can now be planted up for flowering indoors from early winter onwards. Bulbs for indoor 'forcing' are persuaded to flower earlier than they would outside by being subjected to a period

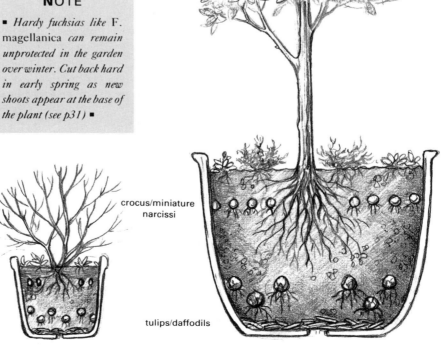

crocus/miniature narcissi

tulips/daffodils

in cold, dark conditions. A wide range of bulbs can be used, but hyacinths, daffodils and crocus are amongst the most reliable.

■ Prepare pots by placing a few crocks over the drainage holes and partly fill with a houseplant compost or special bulb fibre.

■ Place the bulbs on top of the compost so their tips are just below the level of the rim. Bulbs should not touch each other or the sides of the pot. One 23cm (9in) pot will take five daffodils or fifteen crocus.

■ Fill in with compost around the bulbs, leaving the tips of hyacinths and daffodils just exposed, and with enough space above the level of the compost to allow for watering.

■ Water thoroughly, and put the pots in a cold, dark place for twelve weeks. If the pots are being kept outside, cover

with black polythene. Water occasionally.

■ When the shoots are at least 5cm (2in) high, bring the pots into a cool, lightly shaded spot until the flower-buds are showing. Then move them to a position in full light.

■ Water regularly, and keep as cool as possible to prolong the flowering period.

### NOTE

■ *Any kind of decorative container can be pressed into service for indoor bulbs. If using a china bowl without drainage holes, it is best to plant in special bulb fibre which contains peat, oyster shell and charcoal to prevent the soil becoming stagnant when watered. Generally, bulbs that have been forced will not flower in following years* ■

## PLANTING EVERGREENS AND CONIFERS

Early autumn is a good time to plant evergreens and conifers, while the weather is showery and before it gets too cold. Follow the instructions for potting up new plants (see p42), making sure the container is large enough to allow for root and top growth. The rootballs of conifers are often wrapped in sacking or mesh, which should be removed before planting.

Rhododendrons, camellias, pieris and other lime-haters should be grown in a peat-based or proprietary ericaceous compost, and watered with rainwater whenever possible.

## PLANTING CLIMBERS

Clematis, honeysuckle, passion flower and summer jasmine can be planted now. These climb by scrambling and twining and will need to be provided with adequate support. Before planting, fix trellis panels or plastic-coated mesh to the wall or fence behind the climber. Once planted, any shoots that are long enough can be tied in to the trellis. (For notes on putting up trellis see p30).

## PLANTING PERENNIALS

Perennials planted now will have the chance to establish themselves before the growing season starts next spring.

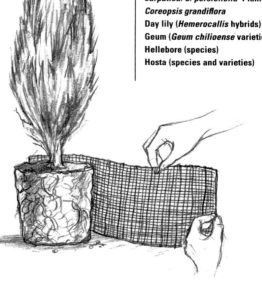

## EVERGREEN SHRUBS AND CONIFERS FOR CONTAINERS

**SHRUBS**
**Bamboo**
*(Arundinaria viridistriata)*
H × S = 60 × 90cm
(2-3ft) × 1m (3ft)
*Berberis buxifolia* 'Nana'
H × S = 45 × 60cm (18 × 24in)
**Box** *(Buxus sempervirens* 'Pyramidalis')* Can be clipped to size and shape
*Lonicera nitida* 'Baggesens Gold' Can be clipped to size and shape
*Fatsia japonica*
H × S = Up to 1.5 × 1.5m (5 × 5ft)

**DWARF-GROWING CONIFERS**
*Juniperus communis* 'Compressa'
H × S = 60 × 15cm (24 × 6in)
*Pinus mugo* 'Humpy'
H × S = 45 × 60cm (18 × 24in)
*Thuja occidentalis* 'Rheingold'
H × S = 90 × 60cm (3 × 2ft)

**KEY**
H × S = height × spread

## PERENNIALS FOR CONTAINERS

*Acanthus mollis*
Campanula *(Campanula arvatica, C. carpatica. C. persicifolia* 'Planiflora')*
*Coreopsis grandiflora*
Day lily *(Hemerocallis* hybrids)
Geum *(Geum chilioense* varieties)
Hellebore (species)
Hosta (species and varieties)

# plants
## OF THE
## *month*
## *1*

### SEDUM
#### species and hybrids

*This group of succulent plants is grown for the fleshy leaves and flat-topped flowerheads, which appear in summer but last right through the autumn. They are tolerant of dry conditions, which make them ideal for containers. Sedums range in size from tiny cushions, suitable for alpine sink gardens, to substantial clump-forming perennials for pots and tubs.*

#### *Sedum acre*

| | |
|---|---|
| type | Evergreen, mat-forming alpine |
| flowers | Yellow; midsummer |
| height | 2.5cm (1in) |
| spread | 30cm (12in) |
| varieties | 'Aureum' has golden tips to the shoots in spring |

#### *Sedum album*

| | |
|---|---|
| type | Evergreen, mat-forming alpine |
| flowers | White on pink stems; midsummer |
| height | 7.5-15cm (3-6in) |
| spread | 38cm (15in) |

#### *Sedum × 'Autumn Joy'*

| | |
|---|---|
| type | Perennial |
| flowers | Pink, fading to orange-brown; early to late autumn |
| height | 60cm (2ft) |
| spread | 45cm (18in) |

*Sedum* 'spectabile'

#### *Sedum reflexum*

| | |
|---|---|
| type | Evergreen, mat-forming alpine |
| flowers | Yellow; midsummer to early autumn |
| height | 15-23cm (6-9in) |
| spread | 30cm (12in) |

#### *Sedum 'Spectabile'*

| | |
|---|---|
| type | Perennial |
| flowers | Pink; early to mid-autumn |
| height | 45cm (18in) |
| spread | 45cm (18in) |

### CULTIVATION
#### *of sedums*

| | |
|---|---|
| planting | Autumn or spring |
| site | Full sun; alpine species in troughs, sinks, shallow pots or strawberry pots; perennial species in large pots or tubs |
| compost | Well-drained, multi-purpose. Alpine species will do best in a gritty, alpine mix (see p20) |
| care | Leave the flowerheads on through the winter. In spring, break off the dead flower stems at the base |
| propagation | Divide and replant in mid-autumn or early spring |

### HEBE
#### Hebe *species*

*Hebes make good container shrubs, having evergreen foliage and bearing pretty lavender flowers from early summer to autumn. Several of the species and hybrids in this group can be recommended; they are generally hardy in all but the coldest areas, although they do prefer a sunny, sheltered position, tucked up against the wall of the house.*

#### *Hebe × andersonii*

| | |
|---|---|
| type | Tender, evergreen shrub with variegated leaves |
| flowers | Lavender; midsummer to mid-autumn |
| height | 1m (3ft) |
| spread | 60-90cm (2-3ft) |

#### *Hebe* 'Autumn Glory'

| | |
|---|---|
| type | Moderately hardy, evergreen shrub |
| flowers | Violet-blue; midsummer to autumn |
| height | 60-90cm (2-3ft) |
| spread | 60-90cm (2-3ft) |

### Hebe 'Bowles Hybrid'

| | |
|---|---|
| type | Moderately hardy, evergreen shrub |
| flowers | Mauve; early summer to early autumn |
| height | 60cm (2ft) |
| spread | 60cm (2ft) |

### Hebe buchananii 'Minor'

| | |
|---|---|
| type | Moderately hardy, dwarf evergreen shrub |
| flowers | White; midsummer |
| height | 5cm (2in) |
| spread | 15cm (6in) |

### Hebe 'Carl Teschner'

| | |
|---|---|
| type | Moderately hardy, evergreen shrub |
| flowers | Violet-blue; midsummer |
| height | 30cm (12in) |
| spread | 60cm (2ft) |

### Hebe pinguifolia 'Pagei'

| | |
|---|---|
| type | Hardy, evergreen, spreading shrub |
| flowers | White; early summer |
| height | 23cm (9in) |
| spread | 1m (3ft) |

## CULTIVATION
*of hebes*

| | |
|---|---|
| planting | Autumn or late spring |
| site | Full sun, sheltered – ideally against a warm wall. Larger types can be grown in tubs, dwarf varieties in troughs |
| compost | Well-drained, multi-purpose |
| care | Trim off flowerheads as they fade. Do not allow the compost to become waterlogged. No regular pruning needed, but if shrubs get leggy, cut back hard in spring |
| propagation | By semi-ripe cuttings in late summer |

## STERNBERGIA
*(Sternbergia lutea)*

Sterbergia looks rather like a crocus, but the vivid yellow flowers mark it out from the true autumn crocus *(C. speciosus)*, which is lilac-blue with yellow anthers, and the colchicum *(Colchicum autumnale)* which is a paler lilac. The sternbergia's leaves appear with the flowers but do not reach full height until the spring. This is an easy-to-grow autumn bulb for pots and windowboxes.

| | |
|---|---|
| type | Bulb |
| flowers | Bright yellow; early to mid-autumn |
| height | 15cm (6in) |
| spread | 15-23cm (6-9in) |
| planting | Mid- to late summer, 10-15cm (4-6in) deep |
| site | Sunny; windowboxes, pots |
| compost | Well-drained, multi-purpose |
| care | Leave bulbs in position after flowering, as they prefer not to be disturbed. Lift and divide only when the clumps become congested |
| propagation | Lift and divide (see Care) in late summer and replant immediately |

*Hebe × andersonii*

# plants
## OF THE
## *month*
## 2

### COTONEASTER
*species and hybrids*

*Greatly prized in the wildlife garden for their abundant autumn and winter berries, many cotoneasters can be grown in containers. Most have evergreen foliage which gives year-round cover, and the flowers, although not particularly showy, are borne in great profusion and can be considered an added bonus.*

#### *Cotoneaster congestus*

| | |
|---|---|
| type | Dwarf, spreading, evergreen shrub |
| flowers | Pink; early summer |
| berries | Red; autumn |
| height | 5-15cm (2-6in) |
| spread | 30-90cm (1-3ft) |

#### *Cotoneaster conspicuus* 'Decorus'

| | |
|---|---|
| type | Evergreen shrub with arching stems |
| flowers | White; early summer |
| berries | Red; early autumn |
| height | 60-90cm (2-3ft) |
| spread | 60-90cm (2-3ft) |

*× hybridus pendulus*

#### *Cotoneaster horizontalis*

| | |
|---|---|
| type | Deciduous wall shrub – leaves turn red in autumn |
| flowers | Pink; early summer |
| berries | Red; early autumn |
| height | To 2m (6ft) |
| spread | 1.5cm (5ft) |

#### *Cotoneaster × hybridus pendulus*

(*NOTE* Often sold grafted on to the stem of *C. frigidus*, to make a small, ornamental tree with weeping branches)

| | |
|---|---|
| type | Evergreen weeping shrub or miniature tree |
| flowers | White; early summer |
| berries | Red; early autumn |
| height | To 3m (10ft) |
| spread | To 2m (6ft) |

#### *Cotoneaster microphyllus*

| | |
|---|---|
| type | Dwarf, spreading, evergreen shrub |
| flowers | White; late spring, early summer |
| berries | Scarlet; mid-autumn to early winter |
| height | 15cm (6in) |
| spread | To 2m (6ft) |

#### *Cotoneaster wardii*

| | |
|---|---|
| type | Spreading, evergreen shrub |
| flowers | White, pink-tinted; early summer |
| berries | Orange-red; early autumn |
| height | To 2.5m (8ft) |
| spread | To 2.2m (7ft) |

### CULTIVATION
*of cotoneasters*

| | |
|---|---|
| planting | Autumn or late winter |
| site | Full sun; *C. horizontalis* will tolerate a shady wall. *C. horizontalis*, *C. wardii* and *C. hybridus pendulus* will need a large, deep half-barrel or tub |
| compost | Loam-based |
| care | No special care needed. Pruning is not necessary unless plants are outgrowing their allotted space. Cut back deciduous species in late winter, evergreens in mid-spring |
| propagation | By semi-ripe cuttings in late summer, or from seed (berries) collected in autumn |

### STERNBERGIA
*(Sternbergia lutea)*

Sterbergia looks rather like a crocus, but the vivid yellow flowers mark it out from the true autumn crocus *(C. speciosus)*, which is lilac-blue with yellow anthers, and the colchicum *(Colchicum autumnale)* which is a paler lilac. The sternbergia's leaves appear with the flowers but do not reach full height until the spring. This is an easy-to-grow autumn bulb for pots and windowboxes.

| | |
|---|---|
| type | Bulb |
| flowers | Bright yellow; early to mid-autumn |
| height | 15cm (6in) |
| spread | 15-23cm (6-9in) |
| planting | Mid- to late summer, 10-15cm (4-6in) deep |
| site | Sunny; windowboxes, pots |
| compost | Well-drained, multi-purpose |
| care | Leave bulbs in position after flowering, as they prefer not to be disturbed. Lift and divide only when the clumps become congested |
| propagation | Lift and divide (see Care) in late summer and replant immediately |

#### *Hebe* 'Bowles Hybrid'

| | |
|---|---|
| type | Moderately hardy, evergreen shrub |
| flowers | Mauve; early summer to early autumn |
| height | 60cm (2ft) |
| spread | 60cm (2ft) |

#### *Hebe buchananii* 'Minor'

| | |
|---|---|
| type | Moderately hardy, dwarf evergreen shrub |
| flowers | White; midsummer |
| height | 5cm (2in) |
| spread | 15cm (6in) |

#### *Hebe* 'Carl Teschner'

| | |
|---|---|
| type | Moderately hardy, evergreen shrub |
| flowers | Violet-blue; midsummer |
| height | 30cm (12in) |
| spread | 60cm (2ft) |

#### *Hebe pinguifolia* 'Pagei'

| | |
|---|---|
| type | Hardy, evergreen, spreading shrub |
| flowers | White; early summer |
| height | 23cm (9in) |
| spread | 1m (3ft) |

### CULTIVATION
*of hebes*

| | |
|---|---|
| planting | Autumn or late spring |
| site | Full sun, sheltered – ideally against a warm wall. Larger types can be grown in tubs, dwarf varieties in troughs |
| compost | Well-drained, multi-purpose |
| care | Trim off flowerheads as they fade. Do not allow the compost to become waterlogged. No regular pruning needed, but if shrubs get leggy, cut back hard in spring |
| propagation | By semi-ripe cuttings in late summer |

*Hebe × andersonii*

# *practical* project

## PLANTING UP A CHIMNEY POT

*POT DÉCOR*
*Chimney pots can be painted with a good exterior-quality house paint, to match or contrast with adjacent walls. A stencil pattern could be applied over the base coat to decorate the sides.*

Out-of-commission chimney pots are popular plant containers for gardens and patios, although their weight makes them unsuitable for balconies. Rooftop gardens – where chimneys rightfully belong – can accommodate them as long as the underlying roof structure is strong. If not, you will have to be content with them at ground level.

Chimney pots tend to look best alongside older Georgian, Victorian or Edwardian buildings, although they are equally at home in an urban or country setting. If possible, buy from a salvage merchant in the area where you live: that way, the style of the pots is more likely to complement the local architecture. Chimney pot connoisseurs can recognise a salt-glaze finish or a particular type of clay at fifty paces, and it is this regional variety that adds greatly to their charm and collectability.

## PRACTICALITIES

It has to be said that chimney pots are not the most practical way to grow plants. As a container, they have several obvious drawbacks:

they have no base, and they are too long and narrow to suit the roots and growing shape of most plants. These problems are not, however, insurmountable. The essential thing to remember is to choose a location for the pot *before* planting, so that it can be put in position and left there more or less permanently. You can, of course, cheat slightly by suspending a smaller pot in the top of the opening, although this does reduce the compost capacity and usually means that the plants are restricted in their growth. A hanging basket – perched on the top and filled with trailing plants that hang down and cover the join between basket and pot – is a reasonable compromise. It is also possible to buy clay containers which look like chimney pots, but have a base with a drainage hole.

## PLANTING

■ Scrub the pot thoroughly with hot water before planting it up to remove any soot or chemical residues.

■ Stand it on a large, shallow tray of pebbles or, alternatively, on a gravel area.

■ Fill the bottom section with clay aggregate pebbles or stone chippings. For economy and convenience, tall pots can be packed with builder's rubble or ballast. This drainage layer will vary in depth according to the height of the pot – a pot 60cm (2ft) high should be filled with one-third drainage material; a pot of 1.2m (4ft) or more will need two-thirds.

■ Place a piece of polythene, with holes punched in it, over the drainage layer.

■ Fill with multi-purpose potting compost and add the plants – trailing types around the outside, bulbs and upright plants in the centre.

■ Firm down and water thoroughly until the water trickles into the pebble-filled tray.

## AFTERCARE

■ Water frequently through the summer and use a liquid feed every two weeks.

■ Remove bedding plants such as begonias and pelargoniums at the end of the summer.

■ Every two to three years, in spring, remove and renew all the plants and add fresh compost.

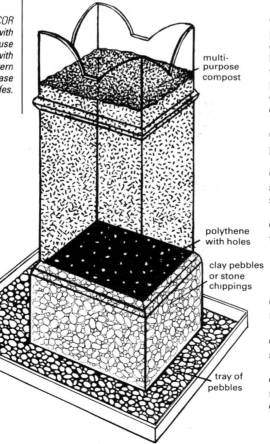

multi-purpose compost

polythene with holes

clay pebbles or stone chippings

tray of pebbles

**PLANTS FOR CHIMNEY POTS**

**BULBS**
**Crocus (Crocus vernus)**
**Dwarf daffodil (Narcissus cyclamineus or N. bulbocodium)**
**Tulip (Tulipa kaufmanniana, T. tarda, T. greigii)**

**TRAILING PLANTS**
**Campanula**
**Ivy-leaved pelargonium (Pelargonium peltatum)**
**Nasturtium**
**Small-leaved ivy (Hedera helix – plain and variegated forms)**

**UPRIGHT PLANTS**
**Begonia**
**Dwarf hebe**
**Hosta**

◄ *SPRING*
Red tulips (Tulipa *'Brilliant Star') and trailing ivy* (Hedera helix). *Plant mid-autumn*

*SUMMER* ►
Sedum acre *and pale pink trailing variegated pelargonium (*Pelargonium *'L'elegante').* *Plant early summer*

◄ *WINTER/EARLY SPRING*
*Variegated trailing ivy (*Hedera helix*), early dwarf daffodils (*Narcissus cyclamineus *'February Gold') and purple crocus (*Crocus vernus *'Purpureus Grandiflorus'). Plant early autumn.*

# plants
## OF THE
## *month*
## 2

### COTONEASTER
*species and hybrids*

*Greatly prized in the wildlife garden for their abundant autumn and winter berries, many cotoneasters can be grown in containers. Most have evergreen foliage which gives year-round cover, and the flowers, although not particularly showy, are borne in great profusion and can be considered an added bonus.*

### *Cotoneaster congestus*

| | |
|---|---|
| **type** | Dwarf, spreading, evergreen shrub |
| **flowers** | Pink; early summer |
| **berries** | Red; autumn |
| **height** | 5-15cm (2-6in) |
| **spread** | 30-90cm (1-3ft) |

### *Cotoneaster conspicuus* 'Decorus'

| | |
|---|---|
| **type** | Evergreen shrub with arching stems |
| **flowers** | White; early summer |
| **berries** | Red; early autumn |
| **height** | 60-90cm (2-3ft) |
| **spread** | 60-90cm (2-3ft) |

× *hybridus pendulus*

### *Cotoneaster horizontalis*

| | |
|---|---|
| **type** | Deciduous wall shrub – leaves turn red in autumn |
| **flowers** | Pink; early summer |
| **berries** | Red; early autumn |
| **height** | To 2m (6ft) |
| **spread** | 1.5cm (5ft) |

### *Cotoneaster* × *hybridus pendulus*

(*NOTE*   Often sold grafted on to the stem of *C. frigidus*, to make a small, ornamental tree with weeping branches)

| | |
|---|---|
| **type** | Evergreen weeping shrub or miniature tree |
| **flowers** | White; early summer |
| **berries** | Red; early autumn |
| **height** | To 3m (10ft) |
| **spread** | To 2m (6ft) |

### *Cotoneaster microphyllus*

| | |
|---|---|
| **type** | Dwarf, spreading, evergreen shrub |
| **flowers** | White; late spring, early summer |
| **berries** | Scarlet; mid-autumn to early winter |
| **height** | 15cm (6in) |
| **spread** | To 2m (6ft) |

### *Cotoneaster wardii*

| | |
|---|---|
| **type** | Spreading, evergreen shrub |
| **flowers** | White, pink-tinted; early summer |
| **berries** | Orange-red; early autumn |
| **height** | To 2.5m (8ft) |
| **spread** | To 2.2m (7ft) |

### CULTIVATION
*of cotoneasters*

| | |
|---|---|
| **planting** | Autumn or late winter |
| **site** | Full sun; *C. horizontalis* will tolerate a shady wall. *C. horizontalis*, *C. wardii* and *C. hybridus pendulus* will need a large, deep half-barrel or tub |
| **compost** | Loam-based |
| **care** | No special care needed. Pruning is not necessary unless plants are outgrowing their allotted space. Cut back deciduous species in late winter, evergreens in mid-spring |
| **propagation** | By semi-ripe cuttings in late summer, or from seed (berries) collected in autumn |

## CUP AND SAUCER VINE
### *(Cobea scandens)*

This vigorous scrambling climber takes its name from the large cup-shaped flowers that are set in a flat, saucer-like green calyx. It has a long flowering period and is invaluable for covering a screen or trellis in one summer. It climbs using tendrils, so will need the support of plastic-coated wire netting or a wooden trellis. It will grow happily in a half-barrel or deep wooden trough, against a balcony wall or patio fence. It is not winter-hardy in all areas, so is usually grown each year from seed.

| | |
|---|---|
| type | Half-hardy perennial (often grown as an annual) |
| flowers | Purple; summer to mid-autumn |
| height | To 6m (20ft) |
| spread | 1m (3ft) |
| planting | Plant out in early to mid-summer |
| site | Full sun, sheltered; against a wall, fence or screen |
| compost | Multi-purpose |
| care | Keep well-watered through the summer months but do not use any fertiliser or feeds. Too many nutrients will encourage stem and leaf growth at the expense of flowers |
| propagation | From seed sown indoors in mid-spring |
| varieties | 'Alba' has green-white flowers |
| note | *Cobea scandens* can be grown as a perennial in a conservatory where the winter temperature does not drop below 8°C (46°F) |

# OCTOBER

*This is a month of changing skies and misty mornings – a sure sign that summer has made its final exit. Autumn is now in full swing and we can expect frosts before the end of the month in many areas. Although the days are undeniably shorter, this is a productive time of year in the container garden and there is no need to turn our backs on the outdoor space just yet.*

*There is still plenty of autumn colour to be seen from shrubs like the acers and climbers such as Virginia creeper – all of which grow happily in tubs. Windowboxes can be colourful too, as* Cyclamen hederifolium *comes into flower along with* Colchicum autumnale. *Annual flowers have just about had their day and can be discarded to make room for displays of spring tulips; biennials such as wallflowers, grown from seed this year, can now be put into their flowering positions. Bulbs and spring-flowering biennials grown together in pots and windowboxes create a pretty, cottage-garden effect.*

*This is a good time to generate new hardy plants, either by dividing existing perennials or by investigating what is on offer at the garden centre. Newly bought plants should not be repotted until the spring, unless they are visibly straining out of their existing pots. If it is absolutely necessary, transfer the plant into a container only very slightly larger than the original – leave any major repotting until the spring, when the root systems can make good growth.*

*For many container gardeners, this month is harvest time, and there are apples and pears to be collected and stored safely away; the old technique of cradling the fruit in the palm of your hand and gently twisting, so that the fruit breaks away with the stalk intact, is still the best way of picking the crop without damage.*

# tasks

## FOR THE

## *month*

**CHECKLIST**

- Cut back and divide perennials
- Take hardwood cuttings
- Begin planting trees, shrubs, roses and tulips
- Continue planting spring-flowering bulbs
- Plant out biennials and perennials
- Choose a compost bin
- Lift begonias
- Tidy alpine sinks
- Take in parsley
- Routine tasks: clear leaves, pull up annuals

sheltered and semi-shaded spot and keep them watered in dry weather.

- The cuttings should be well rooted in about twelve months' time, when they can be repotted into individual pots.

### SHRUBS FOR HARDWOOD CUTTINGS

*Buddleia davidii*
**Honeysuckle** *(Lonicera periclymenum, L. fragrantissima, L. standishii)*
*Philadelphus microphyllus*
*Lonicera nitida*
**Roses**

### CUTTING BACK AND DIVIDING PERENNIALS

As late-flowering perennials die back, the flower stems and top growth should be removed.

If they were not divided in early spring, overcrowded clumps should be divided now (see p30).

### TAKING HARDWOOD CUTTINGS

Many shrubs, evergreen and deciduous, can be propagated from hardwood cuttings taken now and overwintered in a sheltered spot outside. Cuttings of

deciduous shrubs should be taken as soon as leaves fall.

- Cut sections of stem about 6cm (¼in) thick and 20-5cm (8-10in) in length.

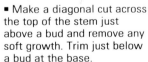

- Make a diagonal cut across the top of the stem just above a bud and remove any soft growth. Trim just below a bud at the base.

- Remove all the lower leaves from evergreens and semi-evergreens, leaving only the top two or three.

- Choose pots at least 25cm (10in) in depth and fill with moist cuttings compost.

- Insert the cuttings around the edge of the pot, about 7.5cm (3in) apart, and with two-thirds of the stem buried.

- Place the pots in a

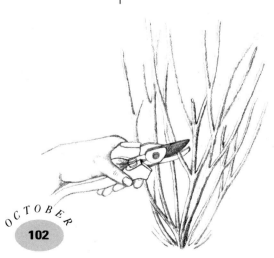

## MAJOR PLANTING SEASON BEGINS

The major planting season for deciduous trees, shrubs and roses begins now while the plants are dormant, and continues until early spring. Bare-rooted plants have to be planted while dormant, although container-grown shrubs and trees can be put in at any time of year. In colder districts, planting of evergreens, which are less hardy, may be better left until spring to avoid frost damage.

### Planting out perennials and biennials

Any annual flowers that remain should now be pulled up. Fork over the compost before filling the spaces with new plants, such as the perennial and biennial plants raised from seed earlier this year (see p50).

### Planting bulbs

Towards the end of the month tulip bulbs can be planted. There is also still time to plant spring-flowering bulbs such as daffodils, crocus, scilla and muscari (see p92)

## CHOOSING A COMPOST BIN

Where space allows, a compost bin makes good practical and economic

### NOTE

▪ *Tulips should be planted at a depth of 15-30cm (6-12in), allowing 10-15cm (4-6in) between each bulb. They prefer a well-drained compost and a sunny position* ▪

sense. Non-diseased clippings and plant waste, as well as vegetable peelings from the kitchen, can all be added to the heap and the resulting compost will provide an excellent mulch and soil conditioner. There are many self-contained bins on the market, usually made of plastic or timber.

It is often recommended that compost heaps be turned from time to time to ensure even decomposition of the contents, but in a confined space this is not likely to be very practical. One solution is to use a compost tumbler – a rotating plastic drum on a stand. This can be tucked away out of sight and should be turned regularly.

## LIFTING AND STORING BEGONIAS

Tuberous begonias (*Begonia* × *tuberhybrida*, Pendula and Multiflora) which have been growing in hanging baskets and tubs should be lifted now and stored away until next spring. If possible, lift the tubers before the first frosts and place them in shallow boxes of dry peat or peat substitute. Choose a place where they can be kept at a minimum temperature of 7°C (45°F) – a spare bedroom, for example – and do not water. In early spring, the tubers will start to produce new shoots – this is the time to bring them into growth again. Set the tubers 7.5cm (3in) apart in seed trays filled with 7.5cm (3in) of moist peat or peat substitute. Bring the trays into a warmer room (about 18°C/64°F) and as the plants develop pot on into suitably sized pots of multi-purpose compost. Do not put begonias outside until late spring or early summer, when there is no danger of frost.

## TIDY ALPINE SINKS AND TROUGHS

Remove any fallen leaves or debris from around alpine plants and heathers – if left, they could cause the plants to rot. Snip off any dead or decaying foliage and cut back any species that are outgrowing their allotted space. Remove weeds by hand and spread a layer of gravel over the surface to prevent the plants coming into contact with the wet compost.

## TAKE IN PARSLEY

Small pots of parsley can be taken indoors to prolong the season of use. Place the pots on a sunny windowsill and keep the compost just moist. Pots left outdoors can be covered with a cloche (or the top half of a plastic drinks bottle, leaving the top off for ventilation). These measures will ensure that the leaves stay fresh and green through the winter.

*CLEARING LEAVES*
*All dead leaves and other plant debris should be cleared from pots to prevent the spread of disease and keep pests at bay.*

*MIXED CONTAINERS*
*If putting new plants into the same container as a large shrub, cut back the shrub to allow light in and give the new plants a head start.*

# plants
## OF THE
## *month*

## MICHAELMAS DAISY
### *(Aster novi-belgii)*

One of the most popular autumn-flowering plants, the michaelmas daisy offers the container gardener a range of colours and a choice of heights – to suit just about every planting situation. Colours are mainly in the pink-purple spectrum, but there are also pure whites and deep blues, making it easy to plan a totally co-ordinated scheme.

| | |
|---|---|
| type | Herbaceous perennial |
| flowers | Pink, purple, blue, white; early to mid-autumn |
| height | Dwarf: 23-45cm (9-18in) |
| | Tall: 45-90cm (18in-3ft) |
| spread | Dwarf: 15-30cm (6-12in) |
| | Tall: 30-8cm (12-15in) |
| planting | Autumn or spring, allowing room for eventual spread. Michaelmas daisies look best massed together in groups |
| site | Sunny; tall varieties in large pots and half-barrels, dwarf varieties in smaller pots and windowboxes |
| compost | Well-drained, multi-purpose |
| care | Do not allow the compost to dry out, while the plants are in flower. Give a liquid feed once a week from midsummer until flowering has finished. Support taller varieties with canes, link stakes or twiggy sticks. Michaelmas daisies tend to deteriorate after two or three years: lift the plants |

and discard the old, central part of the clump, replanting the healthy outer parts

| | |
|---|---|
| propagation | Divide plants in early spring, replanting only the healthy roots, ie those with new shoots (see Care) |
| varieties | *Tall:* 'Winston S. Churchill' – ruby red 75cm (2½ft) |
| | 'Chequers' – violet 75cm (2½ft) |
| | *Dwarf:* 'Little Pink Beauty' – pink 38cm (15in) |
| | 'Lady in Blue' – blue 25cm (10in) |
| | 'Professor Kippenburg' – mauve 23cm (9in) |
| | Mixed colours are also available |
| related species | *Aster alpinus* is a dwarf, spreading perennial, suitable for windowboxes and pots. It grows to 15cm (6in), spreading to 30cm (12in) or more. 'Beechwood' is a mauve variety; 'Wargrave Variety' is pink |

## COLCHICUM
### *(Colchicum autumnale)*

Colchicum is often known as the autumn crocus, but is not in fact related to the true autumn crocus *(Crocus speciosus)*. The two look very similar, although colchicums have longer, broader leaves than the crocus. *C.autumnale* gives a bright splash of colour at the tail end of the year, with several lilac-coloured flowers produced from each corm.

| | |
|---|---|
| type | Corm |
| flowers | Pink or lilac; autumn |
| height | Flowers: 15cm (6in); leaves: 20-5cm (8-10in) |
| spread | 23cm (9in) |
| planting | Late summer; 7.5cm (3in) deep, 23cm (9in) apart |
| site | Sunny; in pots and windowboxes |
| compost | Multi-purpose |
| care | No special care needed |
| propagation | Lift in early summer, separate offsets from the parent bulbs and replant. The offsets may take a year or two to reach flowering size |
| varieties | 'Roseum-plenum' is a double variety with rose-pink flowers |
| related species | 'Album' has small white flowers. *C. speciosum:* flowers 15cm (6in), leaves 30cm (12in); autumn. Hybrids include 'Violet Queen', a deep purple with white lines on the petals |

## JAPANESE MAPLE
### *(Acer palmatum)*

The main attraction of the Japanese maple is the flaming autumn foliage, in colours ranging from crimson to scarlet, bronze and purple. The leaves are deciduous, so it is best grown in a large tub, underplanted with winter and early spring bulbs.

| | |
|---|---|
| type | Deciduous, slow-growing shrub |
| height | To 5m (15ft), named varieties are more compact, to 2.5m (8ft) |
| spread | To 2.5m (8ft) |
| planting | Autumn or spring |
| site | Sun or partial shade, sheltered from winds; in large tubs or barrels |
| compost | Moist, loam-based |
| care | Keep compost moist. In spring, mulch the surface with well-rotted manure, peat substitute or proprietary mulch mix to keep the roots cool |
| varieties | 'Dissectum' has finely divided leaves; 'Dissectum Atropurpureum' has deep purple leaves; 'Viride' has bright green foliage; 'Aconitifolium' turns gold and crimson in autumn |

## CYCLAMEN
### *(Cyclamen hederifolium)*

The delicate pink flowers of the autumn cyclamen look particularly effective planted beneath a deciduous shrub (such as lilac) in a large tub or barrel. They will steal the show in autumn, as the shrub is losing its foliage. In spring, the new growth on the shrub will offer vital shade to the cyclamen during the summer months.

| | |
|---|---|
| type | Corm |
| flowers | Pink, mauve; late summer to late autumn |
| foliage | Deep green with silver markings |
| height | 15cm (6in) |
| spread | 15cm (6in) |
| planting | Late summer, 2.5cm (1in) deep, just covering the corms with compost. Plant 15cm (6in) apart, in groups |
| site | Full or partial shade; sheltered from winds |
| compost | Multi-purpose |
| care | Mulch with 2.5cm (1in) of leaf mould after flowers have finished |
| propagation | From seed collected in autumn |

| | |
|---|---|
| varieties | 'Album' is a white variety |
| related species | *Cyclamen coum* is a miniature, winter-flowering species, which starts flowering in midwinter and lasts until early spring. Height 7.5cm (3in). Flowers: pink; leaves: green, silver-marbled. |

*Cyclamen repandus* is the spring-flowering species, coming into bloom in mid-spring and, if the weather is not too hot, continuing until early summer. The flowers are a deep rose-pink and are sweetly scented. The plant is a similar size to *C. hederifolium*, 15cm (6in) high, and has mottled silver and green leaves which are red underneath.

*Cyclamen persicum* is best known as an indoor, flowering, winter pot-plant. The dark-green rounded leaves are the perfect foil to the vivid colours – pink, white or red, depending on the variety. These plants will not survive the winter outdoors, but equally they need a cool temperature indoors – no more than 15°C (59°F) – an unheated bedroom or hallway is ideal. Stand the pots on trays of gravel topped up with water to prevent the air from drying out around them.

# *practical*
# project

## PLANNING AND
## PLANTING A
## WINTER DISPLAY

Many gardeners think of containers as suitable only for spring and summer bedding. When winter comes, pots and windowboxes are abandoned and, more often than not, plants are left to fade and grow untidy. A little time spent replanting in the autumn pays real dividends, making the outdoor space a good deal more inviting through the otherwise dreary months ahead.

The choice of plants is obviously not as wide as it is in the spring, but there are several alternative approaches. You can either create permanent displays, using evergreen shrubs and hardy trailers, or you can opt for a temporary show of winter bedding such as pansies and primulas, giving way to a succession of late winter and spring bulbs.

### PLANTING SCHEMES

### Windowboxes
Plant a bottom layer of tulips (which don't mind being planted deeply) overlayed with earlier-flowering snowdrops or *Iris reticulata*. Permanent greenery can be provided by low-growing heathers and hardy ivies or trailing periwinkle *(Vinca minor)* – the larger *Vinca major* is too vigorous for windowboxes or hanging baskets.

### Hanging baskets
Trailing ivies provide the mainstay of a winter basket, but colour can be added with the spreading evergreen *Gaultheria procumbens*, which has bright red berries, or a temporary display of purple pansies. Winter pansies will carry on flowering in all but the hardest frosts.

### Permanent tubs
Large evergreen shrubs such as the dramatic New Zealand flax *(Phormium tenax)* or *Yucca gloriosa* can be underplanted with winter bedding pansies or spring-flowering primulas and polyanthus. Other shrubs like holly, with its red berries and camellia with its late-winter flowers, really don't need any adornment.

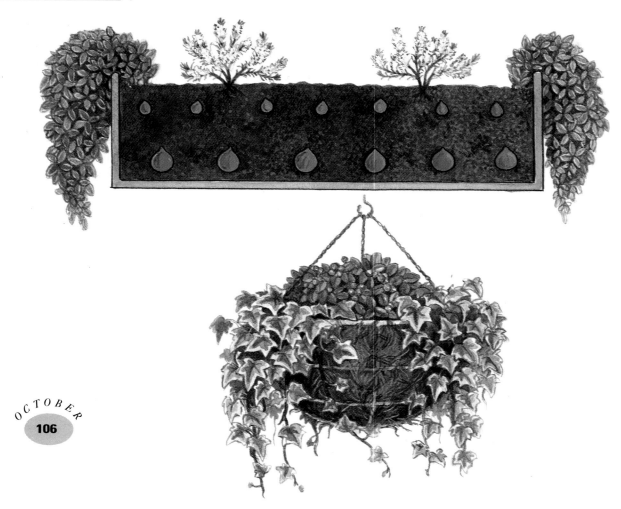

### Individual pots

Plant smaller pots with individual box or bay trees which can be clipped into neat, symmetrical shapes. Alternatively, use a gritty, well-drained compost for a permanent combination of sedums and creeping thyme.

### PLANTING

Aim to have winter containers planted up before the first frosts arrive. The plants will have a better chance of getting to full size or coming into flower – once the frosts arrive, growth slows down dramatically.

For full planting instructions, see p65 (windowboxes), p42 (pots, tubs and other containers) and pp55-6 (hanging baskets).

### CARE OF WINTER CONTAINERS

Check the compost regularly for watering – particularly hanging baskets, which dry out quickly, and any containers which are over-hung by masonry or other buildings and therefore receive no natural rainwater. Plants obviously need less water now than in summer, but the compost should not be allowed to dry out completely. Conversely, it is very important to avoid waterlogging, particularly in the depths of winter, when the temperature can cause the water in the compost to freeze, killing roots and cracking pots. Bedding plants like pansies will benefit from a controlled-release fertiliser, available as pellets or sachets to encourage healthy growth.

*practical*
# project

### PLANNING AND
### PLANTING A
### WINTER DISPLAY

## PLANTS TO CHOOSE FOR A WINTER DISPLAY

### WINTER BEDDING

**Winter pansies (*Viola × wittrockiana* 'Universal')**

### WINTER PERENNIALS

**Bergenia (*Bergenia cordifolia* 'Purpurea')**
**Christmas rose (*Helleborus niger*) E** (white flowers with golden anthers)
**Lenten rose (*Helleborus orientalis*)** – evergreen in mild areas (flowers vary from white to deep pink)

### WINTER-FLOWERING SHRUBS

**Heather (*Erica carnea* 'Springwood White' or 'Winter Beauty')**
***Mahonia japonica* E** (lemon yellow, scented flowers)
***Viburnum tinus* E** (pink budded flowers, opening to white)

### SPRING BEDDING

**Dwarf wallflowers (*Cheiranthus cheiri* 'Tom Thumb Mixed')**
**Polyanthus (*Primula vulgaris* hybrids)**

### SPRING BULBS

**Chionodoxa (*Chionodoxa luciliae, C. gigantea*)**
**Hyacinths (*Hyacinthus orientalis*)**
**Narcissus (*Narcissus cyclamineus, N. jonquilla, N. tazetta* and varieties, eg 'Minnow', 'February Gold')**
**Tulips (*Tulipa greigii, T. foresteriana, T. kaufmannia* and varieties)**

### EVERGREEN TRAILERS/SPREADERS

***Gaultheria procumbens*** (prefers an acid growing medium, but will tolerate a multi-purpose compost)
**Ivy (*Hedera helix*, especially variegated varieties)**
**Lesser periwinkle (*Vinca minor* – 'Aureo-variegata'** has blue flowers and yellow-variegated leaves;
**'Alba'** has white flowers)
***Sedum reflexum*** (looser, more trailing habit than ***Sedum acre***)
**Stonecrop (*Sedum acre* – 'Aureum'** has yellow-tipped shoots) – mat-forming
**Thyme (*Thymus vulgaris* or lemon-scented *T. × citriodorus*)**

### EVERGREENS FOR PERMANENT DISPLAYS

**Bay (*Laurus nobilis*)**
**Box (*Buxus sempervirens* – 'Suffruticosa'** is a dwarf variety; **'Pyramidalis'** can be clipped to shape)
**Camellia (*Camellia japonica*)**
**Euonymus (*Euonymus japonicus* 'Microphyllus'** – **'Aureus'** has yellow leaves; **'Variegatus'** has white
margins to the leaves)
**Holly (*Ilex aquifolium* 'Aureo-marginata')**
**Mahonia (*Mahonia aquifolium*)**
**Mexican orange blossom (*Choisya ternata*)**
**New Zealand flax (*Phormium tenax* – 'Purpureum'** has purple leaves; **'Variegatum'** has bold cream stripes)
**Pieris (*Pieris formosa* var. *forestii, P.* 'Wakehurst')**
**Spotted laurel (*Aucuba japonica* 'Maculata')**
***Yucca gloriosa***

### WINTER BULBS

**Crocus (*Crocus chrysanthus*)**
**Iris histrioides major**
**Iris reticulata**
**Snowdrops (*Galanthus nivalis*)**

### DWARF CONIFERS

***Chamaecyparis pisifera* 'Nana'**
***Juniperus communis* 'Compressa'**
***Pinus mugo* 'Gnome'**
***Thuja occidentalis* 'Caespitosa'**

Stonecrop

Camellia

Yucca gloriosa

Ivy

Tulipa gregii

Lenten rose

# NOVEMBER

*This month conjures up pictures of fallen leaves and bonfires – not something the container garden really has to contend with. Yet the traditional calendar of activities goes on, and this is certainly the time for sweeping, tidying and protecting plants in preparation for winter.*

*When the weather brings more than its fair share of cold, rainy days, it is some consolation to think about the flowers you will be enjoying in the summer. Lilies, which can be planted now, provide a legitimate excuse for dreaming ahead to next year's sunshine. If local garden centres and stores don't stock a good range of species, use one of the specialist nurseries (see Useful Addresses).*

*As deciduous trees and shrubs lose their leaves and herbaceous perennials die back, this is a good time to look at the structures of the garden. Support wires and trellis should be checked for damage and replaced or repaired as necessary. It is also a good idea to scrub down patio furniture and windowboxes, placing them under cover until the spring. Wooden chairs, tables and planters can be painted, varnished or treated with wood preservative to prolong their life.*

*It is still not too late to plant up containers to provide some shape and colour through the winter months ahead. Spring bulbs, particularly tulips, are still available and if planted by the end of the month should bloom successfully. For instant colour, winter-flowering pansies can be interplanted with dwarf conifers and trailing ivy to provide a reliable, trouble-free display.*

# plants
### OF THE
## *month*

## SWEET BAY
### (*Laurus nobilis*)

These hardy shrubs are most often grown as standards and can be seen in pairs, standing like sentries outside the entrance doors of smart town houses. Bay looks best grown in a classic Versailles tub, yet its smart looks belie the fact that it is also a very useful culinary herb, particularly for adding flavour to Mediterranean-style dishes.

| | |
|---|---|
| type | Evergreen shrub, usually grown as a standard |
| flowers | Inconspicuous yellow-green; mid-spring |
| leaves | Glossy, dark green, aromatic |
| height | 2.5m (10ft) |
| spread | 60cm-2.2m (2-8ft) – spread is controlled by clipping |
| planting | Early to mid-spring |
| site | Sun or light shade; sheltered position; in Versailles tubs, half-barrels or large terracotta pots – at least 38cm (15in) diameter |
| compost | Loam-based |
| care | Water well in dry periods. Apply a layer of mulch (well-rotted manure or garden compost) in mid-spring. Trim to shape with secateurs in early summer and again in late summer |
| propagation | By semi-ripe cuttings in late summer |
| varieties | 'Aurea' has golden-yellow leaves |

## COMMON BOX
### (*Buxus sempervirens*)

This is one of the best evergreen shrubs for clipping into symmetrical shapes. A row of clipped box trees, grown in terracotta pots, gives the container garden a formal look and can be used to create a screen between your living space and the outside world. Because it is slow growing, even quite large specimens can be grown permanently in containers. Dwarf varieties will give structure to winter windowboxes.

| | |
|---|---|
| type | Evergreen shrub |
| flowers | Inconspicuous pale green, scented; mid-spring |
| leaves | Glossy, dark green |
| height | To 3m (10ft) – can be reduced by annual clipping |
| spread | To 2m (6ft) – can be reduced by annual clipping |
| planting | Early autumn or spring; in tubs, troughs, pots, windowboxes |
| site | Sun or partial shade |
| compost | Well-drained, multi-purpose |
| care | Water freely in dry weather. Clip to shape in late summer or early autumn. Repot every two years |
| propagation | By semi-ripe cuttings in late summer |
| varieties | 'Suffruticosa' – dwarf (to 45cm/18in); 'Latifolia maculata' – compact (to 1-2m/3-6ft), variegated yellow leaves; 'Pyramidalis' – erect habit, suitable for clipping into a pyramid shape |

## TRAINING A BAY TREE AS A STANDARD

*Allow the central shoot of a young plant to grow 15cm (6in) taller than the desired height of the standard. Remove side shoots lower down the stem as they appear. When the central stem is at the correct height, pinch out the growing tip and pinch out the laterals at the top of the plant to four or five leaves. Continue pinching back until a solid head-shape is formed.*

*In subsequent years, trim twice – in early and late summer – using secateurs. Remove any shoots arising from the base of the stem as they appear.*

# tasks

## FOR THE

## *month*

## CHECKLIST

- Prune deciduous climbers
- Prune roses
- Check bulbs for indoor flowering
- Continue planting tulip bulbs
- Tidy water garden
- Protect plants and pots against frost

### PRUNING OVERGROWN CLIMBERS

■ The tangled growth of bulky honeysuckle can be thinned by cutting out whole stems to ground level. Tie in loose stems to trellis or wires.

■ If it is getting out of hand, Virginia creeper can be trimmed back. Pull the cut growth away carefully so as not to detach the whole lot from the wall.

■ Ivy can be cut back, and dead leaves and stems removed from underneath.

■ Wisteria should be pruned again (see p72) to encourage flowering next year. Cut back all side growth to within two or three buds of last year's growth.

### PRUNING ROSES

Roses can be pruned at any time between now and early spring, while they are dormant. Some roses need more severe pruning than others, but to keep them healthy and flowering well all roses are likely to need some basic pruning. This involves cutting out dead, diseased or damaged wood, and weak and spindly stems.

### Large-flowered bushes (hybrid teas), cluster-flowered bushes (floribundas), patio and miniature roses

The general aim of pruning is to keep bushes 'open' by removing overcrowded and crossing branches from the centre.

■ First, cut out any dead or diseased stems, pruning back to strong, healthy wood.

■ Next, remove any thin, weak stems and any that are crossing over or rubbing against other stems.

■ Finally, cut back the main growing stems – light pruning would be shortening the stems by one-third, hard pruning by two-thirds.

### Standard roses

Main stems on the head should be cut back by up to half their length to maintain a balanced shape.

### Climbing roses

Side stems should be cut back to within two or three buds of where they meet the main stems.

## NOTE

■ *A useful guideline for pruning roses is that the harder the pruning the more growth is stimulated, so weaker stems should be cut back more severely than those which are growing strongly* ■

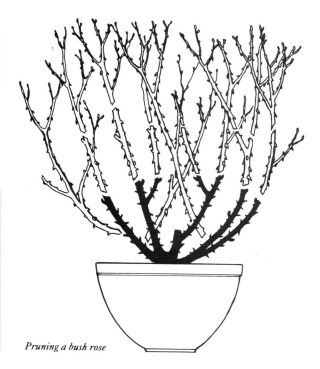

*Pruning a bush rose*

**NOTE**

■ *When pruning roses cuts should always be made at an angle just above an outward-facing bud* ■

### CHECKING BULBS FOR INDOOR FLOWERING

Take a look at your pots of bulbs for indoor flowering. If the shoots are 5cm (2in) high or more, they should be brought into the light (by removing the black polythene, if used), but still kept in a cool place.

Watering should be increased, and once flowerbuds have formed the pots can be placed where they are to flower. Cooler

temperatures will keep the bulbs in flower longer.

### TIDYING WATER GARDENS

Dead leaves should be cleared regularly from the water surface. Underwater oxygenating plants should be thinned out and any debris removed from the bottom of the pool.

### WINTER PROTECTION

Pot-grown plants are more susceptible to frost damage than those grown in the soil, and those in small pots are particularly vulnerable.

■ If practical, small pots can be gathered together and plunged up to their rims in a larger container of compost.

■ Large pots can be wrapped in bubble polythene or a thick layer of newspaper.

■ The protection should be wrapped around the sides of

the pot, leaving the base and drainage holes uncovered.

■ Remove saucers from beneath pots to prevent water gathering and forming ice.

■ Wherever practicable, pots should be lifted off the ground on bricks or 'pot feet'. These measures will also help to protect terracotta pots against frost damage.

*PROTECT YOUR POTS*

*Some decorative terracotta pots are not reliably frostproof. Those with narrow or tapered necks are most at risk, since when soil freezes it expands and is forced upwards. Wiring pots around the rim will help reinforce them where they are most likely to crack.*

# plants

## OF THE

## *month*

## SWEET BAY
### *(Laurus nobilis)*

These hardy shrubs are most often grown as standards and can be seen in pairs, standing like sentries outside the entrance doors of smart town houses. Bay looks best grown in a classic Versailles tub, yet its smart looks belie the fact that it is also a very useful culinary herb, particularly for adding flavour to Mediterranean-style dishes.

| | |
|---|---|
| type | Evergreen shrub, usually grown as a standard |
| flowers | Inconspicuous yellow-green; mid-spring |
| leaves | Glossy, dark green, aromatic |
| height | 2.5m (10ft) |
| spread | 60cm-2.2m (2-8ft) – spread is controlled by clipping |
| planting | Early to mid-spring |
| site | Sun or light shade; sheltered position; in Versailles tubs, half-barrels or large terracotta pots – at least 38cm (15in) diameter |
| compost | Loam-based |
| care | Water well in dry periods. Apply a layer of mulch (well-rotted manure or garden compost) in mid-spring. Trim to shape with secateurs in early summer and again in late summer |
| propagation | By semi-ripe cuttings in late summer |
| varieties | 'Aurea' has golden-yellow leaves |

## COMMON BOX
### *(Buxus sempervirens)*

This is one of the best evergreen shrubs for clipping into symmetrical shapes. A row of clipped box trees, grown in terracotta pots, gives the container garden a formal look and can be used to create a screen between your living space and the outside world. Because it is slow growing, even quite large specimens can be grown permanently in containers. Dwarf varieties will give structure to winter windowboxes.

| | |
|---|---|
| type | Evergreen shrub |
| flowers | Inconspicuous pale green, scented; mid-spring |
| leaves | Glossy, dark green |
| height | To 3m (10ft) – can be reduced by annual clipping |
| spread | To 2m (6ft) – can be reduced by annual clipping |
| planting | Early autumn or spring; in tubs, troughs, pots, windowboxes |
| site | Sun or partial shade |
| compost | Well-drained, multi-purpose |
| care | Water freely in dry weather. Clip to shape in late summer or early autumn. Repot every two years |
| propagation | By semi-ripe cuttings in late summer |
| varieties | 'Suffruticosa' – dwarf (to 45cm/18in); 'Latifolia maculata' – compact (to 1-2m/3-6ft), variegated yellow leaves; 'Pyramidalis' – erect habit, suitable for clipping into a pyramid shape |

## **T**RAINING A BAY TREE AS A STANDARD

*Allow the central shoot of a young plant to grow 15cm (6in) taller than the desired height of the standard. Remove side shoots lower down the stem as they appear. When the central stem is at the correct height, pinch out the growing tip and pinch out the laterals at the top of the plant to four or five leaves. Continue pinching back until a solid head-shape is formed.*

*In subsequent years, trim twice – in early and late summer – using secateurs. Remove any shoots arising from the base of the stem as they appear.*

## WINTER PANSIES
(*Viola × wittrockiana* 'Universal')

Winter pansies are the same species as the summer-flowering varieties, but the 'Universal' strain has been bred to withstand low temperatures. They are sown in early summer and grown on until sold to the garden centres as bedding plants in the autumn. Generally they are yellow or deep purple, both good, strong, cheerful colours for grey winter days and the perfect antidote to evergreens like ivy and box which, although indispensable, can become monotonous when planted alone.

| | |
|---|---|
| type | Hardy annual |
| flowers | Deep violet, purple, yellow, some with 'faces' or markings; mid-autumn to late winter |
| height | 15-20cm (6-8in) |
| spread | 15cm (6in) |
| planting | Early to mid-autumn, before the first frosts |
| site | Sun or partial shade; pots, windowboxes, hanging baskets |
| compost | Multi-purpose |
| care | Keep compost moist, but avoid waterlogging. Snip off the faded flowers to prolong flowering |
| propagation | Sow seeds in early to midsummer in trays of seed compost. Keep moist and shaded from the sun. Transplant seedlings into individual pots and put into flowering positions in early autumn |

## JUNIPER
(*Juniperus communis*)

The common juniper is a hardy bush which will tolerate most growing conditions, particularly dry, exposed or windy situations. The named varieties are a better choice for a small space, although the species can be grown in a large tub or barrel. Junipers require virtually no attention and can be left in place for years.

| | |
|---|---|
| type | Evergreen conifer |
| foliage | Grey-green |
| height | To 3m (10ft) |
| spread | 2m (6ft) |
| planting | Mid-spring; pots, tubs, troughs |
| site | Sun or light shade; will tolerate exposed sites |
| compost | Well-drained, loam-based |
| care | No special care required |
| propagation | By cuttings in autumn |
| varieties | The dwarf variety (*Juniperus communis* 'Compressa') looks effective planted in rows of three in windowboxes or troughs. It reaches a height of 60cm (2ft), but is only 15cm (6in) wide. 'Hibernica' is slow-growing and has blue-grey foliage |
| related species | *Juniperus squamata* 'Blue Star' is a low-growing dwarf conifer, suitable for a stone trough, where it will make neat hummocks of silvery-blue foliage. It grows to a height of 30cm (12in) and spreads to 45-60cm (18-24in) |

# *practical*
# project

## GROWING LILIES
## IN POTS

*Turk's cap*

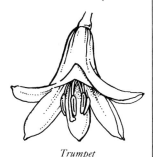

*Trumpet*

### LABEL LILIES
*Remember to keep the lilies' botanical labels, particularly when planting in autumn. With such a long gap until they flower, it is easy to forget which species or hybrid was planted. This is especially important when it comes to propagation.*

Easy to grow and with over eighty species and thousands of hybrids to choose from, lilies are a good subject for beginners and experienced gardeners alike. They adapt well to container growing and are among the most graceful of summer-flowering plants – some the height of understated elegance, others shamelessly dazzling and exotic. Even people with gardens often choose to grow lilies in pots and tubs on the patio, to enjoy the full benefit of their colour and fragrance. Lilies to be displayed in large tubs can be grown on in small pots and put into their permanent sites in late spring.

### BUYING LILY BULBS

Lilies are best bought in autumn when the bulbs have just been lifted, as they deteriorate quickly once out of the ground. However, major garden centre suppliers often do not offer lilies for sale until late winter or early spring – this is acceptable if they have just been lifted, but if they have been stored since autumn they may be in poor condition. The safest way is to order from specialist nurseries (see Useful Addresses) in late summer and plant them as soon as they arrive in the autumn. If you *are* buying bulbs in spring, or indeed at any time, check that they are firm and plump, and reject any that are shrivelled or show signs of mould.

### POTTING UP LILY BULBS

Use deep pots – at least 30cm (12in) and preferably more. Clay pots are better than plastic, as they are heavier and therefore less likely to topple over when the lilies reach full height. They are also less likely to become waterlogged. A 15cm (6in) diameter pot will hold one lily bulb, but they look better planted in groups of three or five in large pots.

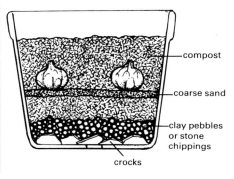

compost

coarse sand

clay pebbles or stone chippings

crocks

■ Cover the drainage hole with broken crocks and add a 5cm (2in) layer of clay pebbles or stone chippings.

■ Fill with a layer of compost to the required depth (see Planting Depth). Use loam-based or multi-purpose potting compost.

■ Add a 2.5cm (1in) layer of coarse sand or grit and place the bulbs on this, spreading out the roots. Set them 15cm (6in) apart.

■ Top-up to the rim with more compost, leaving a gap of 2.5cm (1in) between the compost and the rim for watering. Water in.

### AFTERCARE

■ *Autumn* If planting the bulbs in autumn, stand the pots under shelter to prevent too much heavy rain soaking the compost.

■ *Spring* If planting in spring, stand the pots in a lightly shaded position until the plants have made good growth. Autumn-planted bulbs should also be moved out into a lightly shaded position.

■ *Early summer* Bulbs grown in individual pots can be transferred to larger pots and tubs. Move all pots into their permanent positions when the stems are well developed – a sunny spot is ideal, but lilies will also grow in light shade.

■ *Summer* Turn the pots weekly to ensure that the stems grow straight. Tie taller varieties to bamboo canes, taking care not to spear the bulbs – placing the cane 5-7.5cm (2-3in) away from the stem should be safe. Start feeding when the buds are visible. Apply a liquid feed once every two weeks and continue for a month after the flowers fade.

■ *Late summer* When the leaves start to wither, reduce watering, but do not let the compost dry out altogether.

### IN SUBSEQUENT YEARS

Lilies grown in small-capacity containers should be repotted each spring in fresh compost. Those in larger tubs and urns can remain in position if the top 5cm (2in) of compost is removed and renewed, to add fresh nutrients.

### INCREASING YOUR STOCK

The simplest way to propagate lily bulbs is by division, but they can also be increased from bulbils and bulblets.

#### Division

Many species and hybrids will naturally produce two stems instead of one every two or three years. Lift these in the autumn and break the two stems apart, replanting immediately. This ensures that the bulbs do not become overcrowded underground and allows you to increase the number of plants at the same time. The new bulbs may take a year or two before flowering.

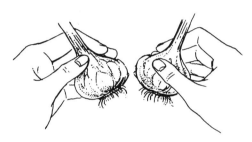

#### Bulbils

Some of the lilies, including *Lilium tigrinum*, *L. speciosum* and *L. bulbiferum* grow stem bulbils – tiny bulbs which form in the leaf axil (the angle between the leaf and the stem).

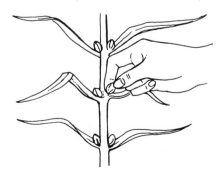

■ Pick off the bulbils in late summer and insert them into a tray or pot of moist potting compost.

■ Cover the surface with horticultural grit and label the pots.

■ Place them in a cold frame or a sheltered porch, where they will be protected from heavy rains.

■ In spring, pot each bulbil into a small pot of potting compost. Bulbils may take two to three years to reach flowering size.

#### Bulblets

Many lilies grow bulblets on the part of the stem *under* the compost.

■ After flowering in late summer or early autumn, lift the lily out of the pot and pick off the bulblets.

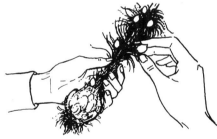

■ Replant the main plant.

■ Plant the bulblets at twice their own depths in pots of moist potting compost.

■ Cover with a layer of horticultural grit and label.

■ Place in a cold frame or sheltered place until the spring. Bulblets may take two years to reach full size.

### LILIES FOR POTS

#### SPECIES
**L. bulbiferum** var. **croceum**
bright tangerine orange
**L. candidum (Madonna lily)**
white, scented trumpet flowers
**L. japonicum**
pink-white, scented
**L. longiflorum**
white trumpet flowers, scented
(half-hardy, best grown in
conservatory or greenhouse)
**L. martagon (Martagon lily)**
pink, purple or white turk's cap
flowers (naturalised in many
parts of Britain)
**L. pyrenaicum (Pyrenean lily)**
bright yellow-green, spotted
turk's cap flowers (naturalised in
many parts of Britain)
**L. regale (Regal lily)**
white, scented trumpet flowers
**L. speciosum**
white-crimson, scented (late
flowering – early autumn, not
advisable where frosts come
early)
**L. tigrinum (Tiger lily)**
orange-red, spotted turk's cap
flowers

#### ASIATIC HYBRIDS
**'Enchantment'** (red)
**'Destiny'** (yellow, spotted with
brown)

#### AURELIAN HYBRIDS
**'Bright Star'** (white, with central
orange star)
**'Golden Splendour'** (gold with
maroon stripe)
**'Green Magic'** (green to white)
**'Pink Perfection'** (strong pink)

### PLANTING DEPTHS

#### DEEP PLANTING
*Most lilies are stem-rooting: that is, they produce feeding roots on the lower part of the stem. They should be planted with 15cm (6in) of soil over them.*

#### SHALLOW PLANTING
*The Madonna lily ((Lilium candidum), the Martagon lily (L. martagon) and the Pyrenean lily (L. pyrenaicum) are bulb-rooting lilies, producing roots only at the base of the bulb. These bulbs should be planted with 5cm (2in) of soil over them.*

# DECEMBER

*As the year hurries to a close, winter descends, sometimes with alarming speed. Frosts are a definite possibility in many areas, yet in milder regions, autumn can linger for a surprisingly long time. The tasks to be undertaken outdoors will be dictated to some degree by the weather, but as long as frost protection is in place, container gardeners can enjoy the seasonal festivities without too much concern for their plants.*

*Traditionally, this is the month for planting bare-rooted roses, shrubs and fruit trees. Although more and more nurseries and garden centres are selling container-grown plants (which can be transplanted at any time of year), some plants are only available bare-rooted and must be potted up while they are dormant. This is really the last chance to plant them before freezing, wet weather makes it impossible. If not, it is advisable to wait until late winter.*

*The winter patio or balcony need not look bare and unloved. Evergreen shrubs and conifers give shape and clothing; there can even be splashes of colour from purple winter pansies, red holly berries and white* Helleborus niger. *Keeping the area swept, and trimming off any dead flowerheads or shrivelled leaves, will ensure it never looks neglected.*

*In mild regions, it is not usually necessary to protect terracotta pots against frost, unless they are particularly valuable antiques or, non-frostproof imports from the Mediterranean. However, in many areas it would be prudent to gather the pots together in the shelter of a porch, or as near to the house wall as possible. If it is not possible to bring large pots indoors, wrap them in plastic bubble-wrap or hessian. Avoid watering unless it is absolutely necessary – it is usually the freezing of wet compost which causes the pots to crack.*

# tasks
## FOR THE
## *month*

## CHECKLIST

- Plant new trees, shrubs and roses
- Clear and sweep patio
- Service tools
- Check plants and pots for frost protection
- Winter-prune fruit trees

### PLANTING BARE-ROOTED PLANTS

Orders received from nurseries can be planted now. Trees, fruit and roses delivered from nurseries at this time of year are dormant and most likely to be 'bare-rooted' – that is, they are dug up from the open ground and sent out without soil, but wrapped in damp straw or other protection to prevent them drying out.

- When the plants arrive, remove the packing and protective covering.

- Examine the roots and use a sharp knife to cut back any which are split or damaged.

- The roots may be dry, so it is always a good idea to place the plant in a bucket of tepid water for about an hour before planting.

### NOTE

- *Before planting bare-rooted trees and shrubs it is important to look for the soil mark on the stem – always plant back at the same level* ■

### Planting method

- Choose a container which has drainage holes and is wide and deep enough to take the full spread of roots comfortably.

- Cover the holes with pieces of broken pot and add a 5cm (2in) layer of stone chippings or clay aggregate pebbles to improve drainage around the roots.

- Add a layer of compost – the exact depth will depend on the size of the roots.

- Hold the shrub in the pot and begin to fill in with compost around the roots.

- Firm the compost down well, adding more if necessary.

### Staking trees and standard roses

Trees and standard roses will need staking at the time of planting. The overall length of the stake should be the height of the stem plus the depth of the container. Put the stake in place at the same time as you position the plant, and secure with proprietary rubber or plastic adjustable ties.

*DELAYED PLANTING*
*If planting is delayed because the weather is frosty, newly-delivered plants can be safely stored for a few days in a cool but frost-free place. The protection should be left around their roots, but the packaging removed from the branches to let air circulate.*

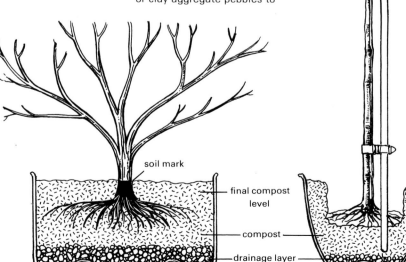

soil mark

final compost level

compost

drainage layer

## CLEANING THE PATIO

Patios should now swept and cleared of leaves and other debris. Dislodge dead leaves from between trellis panels and walls. Clear behind large pots and against walls and fences where snails, wood lice and other pests can lurk and breed undisturbed. Collect up empty plastic pots, and stack lightweight tables and chairs so that they will not be blown about in high winds.

### NOTE

*■ If snow falls brush it off trees and shrubs before the weight can damage their branches ■*

## SERVICING TOOLS

Secateurs and shears can be sent off for sharpening now, so that they will be ready for use in the spring. Bring all tools under cover for the winter.

## WINTER PRUNING OF FRUIT TREES

Apples and pears grown as espaliers or bushes should be pruned this month. Newly-bought trees need to be pruned to train them into their eventual shape; older, established trees should just be pruned lightly to promote growth and keep an attractive shape.

### Bush Tree
■ *Pruning a young (two-year old) bush*
■ Cut back each of the branches to an outward-facing bud. Reduce the

### NOTE

*■ Vulnerable plants and pots should be given extra winter protection (see p113) ■*

length by a half to two-thirds.

■ *Pruning an established bush*
■ The aim is to keep the centre of the bush open, removing any branches which cross over. Lightly cut back the main branches. Reduce laterals (side shoots) to 5-7.5cm (2-3in).

### Espalier
■ *Pruning a young (two- or three-year-old) espalier*
■ Cut back the central stem to a bud 5cm (2in) above the second wire. Cut back the horizontal stems by about half, close to a bud.

■ *Pruning an established espalier*
■ Once the tree has developed the required number of tiers, it should not need much pruning in winter. Cut back the side shoots to within two or three buds of the horizontal stems (this is also done in midsummer, see p72).

## USEFUL EQUIPMENT

**Fork and trowel**

**Secateurs**

**Hose with adjustable spray nozzle**

**Hose reel which can be hung on wall**

**Watering can with rose**

**Stiff broom**

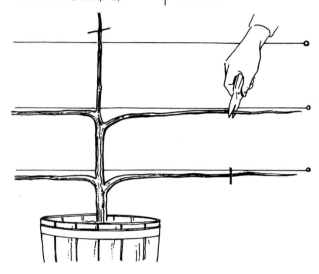

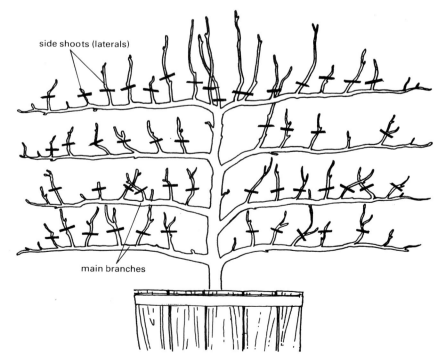

side shoots (laterals)

main branches

# plants
## OF THE
## *month*

## HOLLY
### *(Ilex aquifolium)*

Holly has several merits for the container garden: it is slow-growing and can be clipped to remain compact; it is evergreen and hardy in the most exposed conditions; and, not least, it bears cheerful berries to brighten up the winter scene. Where space is limited, it can be grown as a standard, or, like box, shaped to form a dome of foliage. A row of clipped holly bushes makes an effective (and portable) hedge and, as long as the pots are stable, will stand up to the buffeting winds of rooftop and balcony locations.

| | |
|---|---|
| type | Evergreen shrub or tree |
| flowers | White; mid- to late spring |
| berries | Female trees produce a crop of bright red berries in autumn and winter – a male tree nearby is needed for pollination |
| height | 4m (12ft) |
| spread | 2m (6ft) |
| planting | Plant young specimens in spring or autumn; large pots or tubs |
| site | Sun or shade; variegated forms retain their colour better in a sunny position |
| compost | Moist, loam-based |
| care | Water frequently after planting until the tree is established. Keep well watered in dry weather. No regular pruning is needed, but pinching out the growing tips of young plants in spring will encourage bushy growth. Clip hollies to the desired shape in mid- to late summer (see p51 for training of standard trees) |
| propagation | By semi-ripe cuttings in late summer |
| varieties | Named varieties include 'Argenteo-marginata Pendula' – male and female weeping trees with silver-edged leaves (H: 4m/12ft, S: 3m/10ft); 'J.C. Van Tol' – a column, shaped female tree with glossy green leaves which bears berries without a nearby male tree (H: 3m/10ft, S: 2m/6ft); 'Golden Queen' – a column-shaped male tree with golden-edged leaves (H: 3m/10ft, S: 2m/6ft). 'Ferox' is a bushy, slow-growing male tree with short, sharp spines – hence its common name 'Hedgehog Holly' |

## SKIMMIA
### *(Skimmia japonica)*

Skimmia is a reliable, slow-growing shrub that has something to offer in every season of the year. The scented flowers are borne in short panicles in spring, but the real stars are the brilliant berries which last longer than almost any other fruiting bush. Skimmia tolerates air pollution, which makes it a good choice for town gardens, perhaps used to screen the patio or balcony from a busy road.

| | |
|---|---|
| type | Evergreen shrub |
| flowers | Creamy-white, fragrant; spring |
| berries | Bright red berries; autumn and winter |
| height | 1-1.5m (3-5ft) |
| spread | 1.5m (5ft) |
| planting | Plant in autumn or spring; large pots or tubs |
| site | Sun or partial shade |
| compost | Well-drained, loam-based |
| care | No pruning or special care required |
| propagation | By semi-ripe cuttings in late summer |
| varieties | 'Fragrans' is a strongly fragrant variety; *Skimmia × 'Foremanii'* is slightly more compact than the species (height and spread: 1.2m/4ft) |

## CHRISTMAS ROSE
### *(Helleborus niger)*

The first of the hellebores to come into flower, this is a welcome sight when little else is blooming. The evergreen foliage means the plant can become part of a permanent scheme, perhaps combined with miniature spring bulbs for a long season of interest. The flowers tend to be damaged by wind and rain, although the traditional practice of covering the blooms with transparent cloches seems to defeat the object of having an attractive display. If they can be given any protection – on a sheltered patio for instance – so much the better. For really glossy leaves, choose one of the named varieties such as 'Potter's Wheel'.

| | |
|---|---|
| type | Evergreen perennial |
| flowers | White; early to midwinter |
| height | 30-45cm (12-18in) |
| spread | 30-45cm (12-18in) |
| planting | Mid-autumn; in pots or windowboxes |
| site | Partial shade; sheltered patio or windowledge |

compost | Moist, loam-based
care | Keep well watered through the summer months. Leave the plants in position as long as possible as they resent disturbance. Apply a mulch of well-rotted manure or proprietary mulch mix in spring
propagation | Lift and divide roots in early spring (only when clumps become congested)
varieties | 'Potter's Wheel' has huge white flowers (up to 5in/12cm) across and glossy leaves, but flowers slightly later, in mid- to late winter
related species | Other winter-flowering hellebores make good container plants, particularly the Lenten rose *(Helleborus orientalis)* which has pink or purplish flowers in late winter, and *H. atrorubens*, with its deep plum-coloured blooms from midwinter to early spring

## IVY

### *(Hedera helix)*

The common ivy probably ranks amongst the container gardener's most useful plants. With its self-clinging aerial roots, it can clothe a bare wall or fence with a choice of solid green or variegated foliage. Alternatively, named varieties can be grown in hanging baskets, windowboxes and tubs, where the stems will trail over the sides giving year-round, trouble-free greenery. Ivies thrive in difficult conditions where other plants would fail, but this should not be used as an excuse for neglect. Given a minimum level of care they will respond with glistening, healthy foliage – the perfect backdrop to almost every flowering plant.

type | Evergreen climber/trailer
flowers | Species bears inconspicuous yellow-green flowers; autumn
foliage | Small leaves; colour varies from dark green/to bright yellow, with a range of silver and gold markings
height | Species: to 9m (30ft); named varieties: to 1m (3ft) or more
spread | Species: to 5m (15ft); named varieties: to 1m (3ft)
planting | Spring or autumn
site | Sun or shade; pots, troughs, hanging baskets, windowboxes
compost | Multi-purpose or loam-based
care | Give a liquid feed once a month throughout the spring and summer. Do not allow the compost to dry out altogether. Trim back wall and fence-trained plants in late autumn. Repot small specimens every other year in spring, trimming straggly growth if necessary. Wall-trained plants grown in large tubs should have the top 5cm (2in) of compost renewed each spring
propagation | By hardwood cuttings in mid-autumn
varieties | All suitable for hanging baskets, windowboxes or pots: 'Cristata' – curled, parsley-like leaves; 'Buttercup' – young growth is bright gold; 'Glacier' – silver markings; 'Goldheart' – dark green with a gold centre; 'Tricolor' – silver and pink variegation
related species | The Canary Island ivy *(Hedera canariensis)* has larger leaves and is more suitable for covering walls and fences. *H.c. 'Variegata'* has silver variegation

# *practical* project

### GROWING ROSES IN CONTAINERS

*MINIATURE ROSES*
*Miniature roses are not houseplants – they are hardy, outdoor plants, just like full-sized roses. Many people try to grow them indoors and are disappointed with the results. They can, however, be brought indoors for short periods, particularly if kept in a cool position and not overwatered.*

*PLANTING TIMES*
*Bare-rooted roses can be planted any time from early winter to early spring, while the plant is dormant. Avoid planting when there is a ground frost or heavy rain.*
*Container-grown roses should be planted from early spring onwards, that is, during the growing season. It is best to avoid periods of extreme heat and drought.*

No garden should be without roses, and that includes the tiniest outdoor space or paved area. It is quite possible to grow roses in tubs on patios or in windowboxes, or on balconies and roof gardens. In fact, provided there is a position where the containers can receive sun for at least half the day, roses of some shape or size can be grown.

Traditionalists say that wooden barrels are the only suitable container for roses, but terracotta, stone and other porous materials are equally good – plastic pots or troughs can be used as long as the compost is never allowed to become waterlogged.

The important thing is to give the roses enough space to develop a healthy root system: a minimum depth of 30cm (12in) for the miniature and patio roses, 45cm (18in) for full-size hybrid teas (large-flowered bushes) and floribundas (cluster-flowered bushes). Climbers and ramblers really need a wooden half-barrel or a container of equal capacity if they are to grow healthily.

### CHOOSING ROSES FOR CONTAINERS

#### Miniature roses
Sometimes listed as miniature bush roses, these have been specially developed to cater for smaller gardens and are very well suited to pots and windowboxes. They are tiny versions of the large-flowered and cluster-flowered bushes: the flowers measure up to 5cm (2in) across and the plants themselves are between 23cm (9in) and 38cm (15in) tall. Popular varieties include 'Fire Princess' and 'Angela Rippon'.

#### Patio roses
Officially known as dwarf cluster-flowered bushes, these roses fall inbetween the miniatures and the full-size cluster-flowered types. Their blooms are larger than the miniatures but they still form a compact bush, up to 45cm (18in) high. They are usually too large for windowboxes, but make good subjects for individual pots or planted in groups in troughs or tubs. 'Topsi' is one of the most vivid; 'Sweet Dream' is a more delicate shade.

#### Large-flowered roses (hybrid teas)
The hybrid tea roses are now renamed as 'large-flowered' – which, of course, is their best attribute: large, elegant blooms carried singly, or three or four to a stem. A substantial number of the large-flowered roses can be grown in containers, as long as you select varieties that are not too tall. There are plenty of varieties under 1m (3ft), including 'Just Joey' and 'Pot of Gold'.

#### Cluster-flowered roses (floribundas)
The blooms of the cluster-flowered roses may not be as large or as showy as the large-flowered group, but they bear a greater number of flowers, held in clusters on the stems. The cluster-flowered group also go on flowering more continuously than the large-flowered, which tend to flower in flushes. Suitable varieties for containers include 'Amber Queen' and 'Bright Smile'.

#### Climbers
Climbing roses can happily be grown in large tubs, and trained and pruned to fit the space available. Climbers have stiff, upright stems which will need to be tied in to a support. They look best trained against a wall or fence, on a trellis or horizontal wires. The flowers are generally large, like the large-flowered bushes. 'New Dawn' and 'Golden Showers' will grow to a height of about 2.4m (8ft).

#### Ramblers
Rambling roses have more flexible stems than climbers and look best trained to grow over an arch or pergola. For this reason they are not often grown in containers, but provided they are planted in a large tub or barrel they can be used to create decorative features on a roof garden or paved area. The flowers are borne in clusters, similar to the cluster-flowered bushes. Some varieties can be too vigorous for container growing, but 'Dorothy Perkins' or 'Felicité Perpetué' should stay within bounds.

### PLANTING ROSES

■ Before planting, cut off any dead stems or leaves, and stems that have been damaged. Trim back the roots to about 25cm (10in).

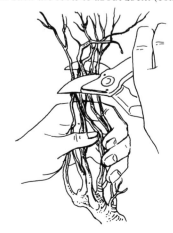

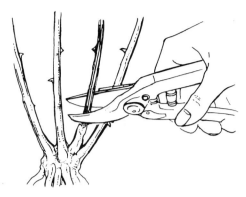

- Cover the bottom 5cm (2in) of the pot with a layer of broken crocks.

- Part-fill the container with multi-purpose potting compost. Position the roots on the compost, ensuring that there is enough room to spread them out. They should not be curled round or touching the outside of the pot.

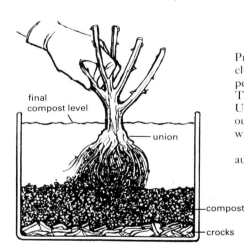

final compost level

union

compost

crocks

- Hold the rose by the stem, positioning it so that the point at which the roots meet the stem (the union) will be just below the surface of the compost. Fill around the roots with more compost, firming it down as you go.

- Fill to just below the rim of the pot with compost. Water lightly and top up with more compost if necessary.

### FEEDING AND WATERING

If planted in winter, roses should not be watered or fed until the following spring. During a normal growing season, roses will need plenty of water, although the compost should never be allowed to remain permanently wet.

A surface mulch of well-rotted manure, garden compost or chopped bark applied in mid-spring will help to stop the compost drying out too quickly. Always water the container *before* applying the mulch. A mulch of manure or compost will feed the plant to some degree, but it is also a good idea to sprinkle a handful of proprietary rose fertiliser around the base of the rose twice a year, in early spring and again in early summer. Water the compost before applying dry fertiliser and fork it in lightly using a hand fork.

### IN SUBSEQUENT YEARS

Repot roses in fresh compost (if necessary) in mid-spring. Large specimens which would be difficult to replant should have the top 5cm (2in) of compost removed and replaced. Continue feeding and watering as above.

### PRUNING

Prune miniatures, patio, large-flowered and cluster-flowered bushes in the dormant period, between late autumn and early spring. The aim is to prune before new growth starts. Use sharp secateurs and always cut to an outward-facing bud. Prune climbers in early winter (see p112).

Prune ramblers in late summer or early autumn.

*DEAD-HEADING*
*All roses should be dead-headed throughout the summer. As individual flowers fade, snip off the heads to the first bud below the flower.*

*Pruning ramblers
(late summer)*

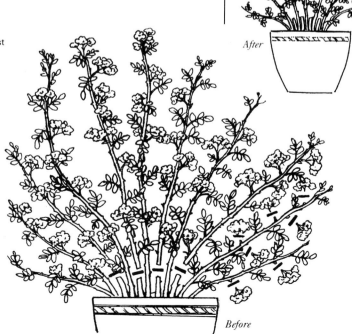

*After*

*Before*

# *practical* project

## GROWING ROSES IN CONTAINERS

### DEALING WITH SUCKERS

*Modern roses have usually been grafted on to a vigorous rootstock to ensure a good root system. This means that occasionally shoots will grow directly from the rootstock underground which are different from the main plant. These are called suckers and should be removed as soon as they appear.*

*Don't cut them off, as this acts as a type of pruning and just encourages them to grow again – simply pull them off instead. The sure way to identify a sucker is to feel under the compost to where it joins the main stem – suckers will come from below the union of the branches and the stem.*

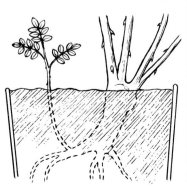

## RECOMMENDED ROSES FOR CONTAINERS

| named variety | type | height | colour | qualities |
|---|---|---|---|---|
| **AMBER QUEEN** | | | | |
| | *Cluster-flowered* | *60cm (2ft)* | *Amber-yellow* | *Fragrant* |
| **ANGELA RIPPON** | | | | |
| | *Miniature* | *30cm (12in)* | *Coral pink* | *Fragrant* |
| **ANNA FORD** | | | | |
| | *Miniature* | *20cm (8in)* | *Deep orange* | |
| **APRICOT SUNBLAZE** | | | | |
| | *Cluster-flowered* | *45cm (18in)* | *Apricot* | *Small flowers* |
| **BRIGHT SMILE** | | | | |
| | *Cluster-flowered* | *60cm (2ft)* | *Yellow* | |
| **DAINTY DINAH** | | | | |
| | *Patio* | *60cm (24in)* | *Coral pink* | *Spreading habit* |
| **FIRE PRINCESS** | | | | |
| | *Miniature* | *45cm (18in)* | *Scarlet* | *Upright* |
| **GOLDEN SHOWERS** | | | | |
| | *Climber* | *2.4m (8ft)* | *Bright yellow* | *Repeat flowering* |
| **ICEBERG** | | | | |
| | *Cluster-flowered* | *1.2m (4ft)* | *White* | *Scented* **Note:** *not the climbing Iceberg* |
| **JUST JOEY** | | | | |
| | *Large-flowered* | *75cm (30in)* | *Copper-pink* | *Flowers 12cm (5in) across* |
| **MME. LOUIS LAPERRIÈRE** | | | | |
| | *Large-flowered* | *75cm (30in)* | *Crimson* | *Scented* |
| **NEW DAWN** | | | | |
| | *Climber* | *3m (10ft)* | *Pink* | *Scented* |
| **PASCALI** | | | | |
| | *Large-flowered* | *60cm (24in)* | *Creamy-white* | *Free-flowering* |

## RECOMMENDED ROSES FOR CONTAINERS

| named variety | type | height | colour | qualities |
| --- | --- | --- | --- | --- |
| PEEK-A-BOO | Patio | 45cm (18in) | Apricot | Small flowers |
| POT OF GOLD | Large-flowered | 1m (3ft) | Yellow | |
| POUR TOI | Miniature | 23cm (9in) | White | Glossy foliage |
| SCARLET GEM | Miniature | 23cm (9in) | Scarlet | |
| STARS N' STRIPES | Miniature | 30cm (12in) | Red and white stripes | Like a miniature Rosa Mundi |
| SWEET DREAM | Patio | 45cm (18in) | Apricot | Scented |
| SWEET MAGIC | Patio | 38cm (15in) | Orange-pink | Scented |
| TOPSI | Patio | 45cm (18in) | Bright red | Repeat flowering |

*NEW ARRIVALS*
*When roses arrive from the nursery, plant them out immediately. If planting is not possible, loosen the packaging around the top growth to allow air to circulate but keep the roots in their original covering. Bare-root roses are usually packed with straw and hessian and, if kept in a frost-free place such as a shed or porch, they should stay in good condition for a week or two.*

*ROOT PROBLEM*
*New roses should never be planted if the roots are dry. If they have dried out during transit, plunge them into a bucket of tepid water for half an hour before planting.*

# appendix
*1*

## GROWING FRUIT AND VEGETABLES IN CONTAINERS

Using pots and windowboxes to grow edible fruit and vegetables is probably the last thing we think of doing – particularly when space is limited. Nevertheless, there is a wide range of kitchen produce which will grow happily in containers given a little extra care. Both vegetables and fruit need a lot of sun and won't thrive in shady basements or passageways. However, many windowboxes, balconies and particularly rooftops do get sun for a large part of the day and this can be utilised to full advantage. Container-grown fruit and vegetables also need regular and consistent watering – if left to their own devices they can dry out and wither remarkably quickly. Likewise, in a confined space the plants use up a lot of nutrients and need regular feeding.

Apart from these basic rules, fruit and vegetables can be treated just like any other patio plants. Grow individual plants in suitably sized pots, or combine three or four plants of the same crop in a larger barrel or trough. Self-watering containers cut down the amount of watering needed, and all pots should be given drip trays.

### GROWING MEDIUM AND FEEDING

A multi-purpose compost will be adequate, or use a loam-based potting compost (see p20) mixed 60/40 with a peat alternative such as coir to retain more moisture. Start to feed the plants about a month after planting, using a liquid feed such as tomato fertiliser or an all-purpose soluble plant food, watered on to the pots about once a week.

### USING GROWING BAGS

Growing bags may not be the most elegant way to display plants, but they certainly do their job as short-term, large capacity containers. The best method of using them is to grow vegetables from seed in small pots (or buy them as small potted plants) and then transplant them into the holes cut into the top of the bags. Most growing bags have instructions on planting, but as a guide an average bag will take three tomato or courgette plants, six cucumbers or peppers, and twelve runner bean plants. Fruit is not really suited to growing bags.

### GROWING FRUIT IN POTS

Most types of fruit can happily be grown in pots and, although the plants are naturally smaller than they would be in the garden proper, the crop can still be quite substantial. Top fruit – apples, pears, plums, cherries and figs – can be trained in a variety of ways to keep the trees contained. Buy only trees grown on dwarfing rootstocks – if in doubt, consult one of the specialist nurseries for advice (see Useful Addresses). If there is room to grow only one variety make sure it is self-fertile (see table). Soft fruit – gooseberries, redcurrants, white currants and compact blackcurrants such as 'Ben Sarek' – can be trained as small bushes and will thrive in pots as long as they are at least 45cm (18in) in diameter. Loganberries and blackberries are generally too large for container growing. Strawberries are ideal for pots, either in conventional terracotta ones or specially designed 'strawberry pots' (see p76).

*Cordon*

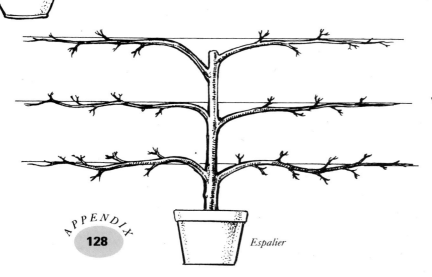

*Espalier*

*Bush*

### FRUIT TREE TRAINING

#### Espalier
This is the way to grow fruit against a wall or in rows. The side branches are trained to grow out along wires in a series of horizontal tiers. Even in a pot, the trees will eventually spread to 3m (10ft) or 5m (15ft) across, so allow plenty of room.

#### Fan
This type of training is only suitable for fruit trees to be set against a wall. The branches of the tree are trained on canes to form the 'ribs' of the fan and are tied in to horizontal wires on the wall. This is a fairly complicated procedure, involving careful pruning and training over several years. However, it is possible to buy three-year-old specimens which already have a good skeleton shape. Allow a space at least 3 × 3m (10 × 10ft) for height and spread.

#### Cordon
This is a smaller version of the espalier, whereby the tree is allowed to produce only one branch or cordon. The usual method is to grow the cordons at an angle, tied in to wires against a wall or in rows. This is a very productive way of growing fruit in a small space, as the containers need only be 1m (3ft) apart.

#### Dwarf pyramid
Dwarf pyramid trees will eventually reach about 1m (3ft), with short branches radiating out from the central trunk. They are ideal on patios or where there is no wall or fence for fruit training, and need only be placed 1.2m (4ft) apart. The branch leaders are cut back each year to keep the tree to manageable proportions.

#### Bush fruit
Apples, pears, gooseberries and currants can be pruned as low-growing bushes, with the branches radiating from the trunk fairly close to the ground. The bush is pruned to keep the centre open in a vase shape, which makes it easier to pick the fruit and prevents the branches becoming overcrowded. Gooseberries and red and white currants can also be grown as cordons.

#### Miniature trees
New research has led to the development of true genetic dwarf trees, which have the same shape as full-sized trees but will only reach about 1.2m (4ft) in height. Dwarf apples, peaches and nectarines are available, all of which are highly suited to container growing on even the smallest patio or balcony.

#### Ballerina™ trees
The most space-saving of all apple trees, the 'Ballerina' has a single upright stem which measures less than 30cm (12in) across, enabling pots to be planted very close together. It will reach an eventual height of 2.2-3m (8-10ft).

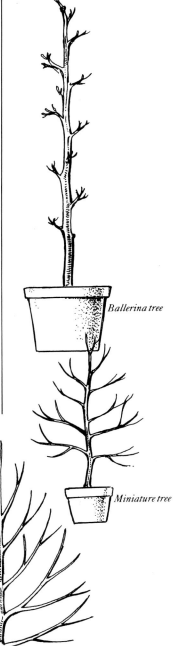

*Ballerina tree*

*Miniature tree*

*Fan*

*Dwarf pyramid*

# appendix

*1*

### RECOMMENDED
### FRUIT AND
### VEGETABLES FOR
### CONTAINERS

## FIG
### (*Ficus carica*)

Figs are well suited to pot growing, as restricting the roots actually encourages short, well-ripened shoots. The plants will produce fruit on a sunny patio or against a warm wall, although the crop will be bigger and better if they can be grown in an unheated conservatory. They can be trained as bush trees or as fans against a wall. The best outdoor variety for growing as a bush is 'White Marseilles', which has pale green fruits in late summer and early autumn. 'Brown Turkey' is best grown under glass or against a sunny wall; it produces brown-green fruits in early autumn.

| | |
|---|---|
| height | 2.5-3m (8-10ft) |
| spread | 2-3m (6-10ft) |
| planting | Plant pot-grown specimens at any time of year from early spring to late autumn. Bare-rooted trees are best planted between late autumn and late winter |
| care | Mulch the surface of newly planted containers with well-rotted manure (this can also be repeated each spring). Water well and start liquid feeding when the fruits begin to swell |
| harvesting | Pick fruits when the stems soften and begin to hang down |

## STRAWBERRY
### (*Fragaria* × *ananassa*)

Strawberry plants produce their fruits in early summer; there are also alpine varieties which have smaller fruit from midsummer to early autumn. 'Cambridge Favourite' is a reliable early summer variety and 'Cambridge Vigour' is particularly good for growing bags. The alpine varieties such as 'Baron Solemacher' form bushy plants without runners. Strawberries can be grown in clay pots, barrels, traditional terracotta strawberry pots (with

planting holes at the side, see p76) or even in hanging baskets – as long as they get plenty of water.

| | |
|---|---|
| height | 20-30cm (8-12in) |
| spread | Up to 30cm (12in) |
| planting | Late summer or early spring (note that those planted in spring will not normally fruit in the first year) |
| care | Keep pots in a light, frost-free place during the winter. If this is not possible, cut back all the foliage and cover the crowns with straw. In the growing season, stand the pots in a sunny position and water reguarly. Use a liquid feed as soon as the fruits start to swell. It is best to discard the plants after two or three seasons and replant |
| harvesting | Pick berries when fully ripe but still firm |

## GRAPE
### (*Vitis vinifera*)

The grape vine climbs by twining tendrils around its support, and produces its fruit in late summer and early autumn. Choose a pot at least 45cm (18in) in diameter and set three canes in a pyramid or wigwam. The young growths can then be trained to grow up the canes, rather like runner beans. Choose a hardy outdoor variety such as 'Seyval Blanc', which is suitable for eating and for wine-making, or 'Brandt', which has sweet black fruit and colourful foliage in autumn.

| | |
|---|---|
| height | 2m (6ft) |
| spread | If trained as a pyramid, no more than 1m (3ft) |
| planting | Late autumn or early spring |
| care | Water well in dry weather and start liquid feeding when fruits start to show. In the first year of fruiting, allow only one bunch of grapes to mature, pinching off any others that start to develop. Once established, in summer cut back all the side shoots that are not bearing fruit to two leaves. Those that have bunches developing should be pinched back to two leaves beyond the fruit. After harvesting, trim back all the side shoots to two buds and remove any weak growth from the top of the vine |
| harvesting | Pick the grapes when they are firm and sweet |

## APPLE
### *(Malus domestica)*

Container-grown apples should be on a dwarfing rootstock (M27 or M9) and can be pruned as espaliers, cordons, dwarf bushes or miniature trees. Recommended varieties include 'Bountiful' for cooking and 'Fiesta' for eating.

height   M27: 2-2.5m (6-8ft);
           M9: 1.2-1.5m (4-6ft); also depends on how it is trained
spread   1-2m (3-6ft)
planting   Container-grown trees can be planted any time between early spring and late autumn. Bare-rooted trees should be put in between late autumn and late winter
care   Water well in spring and summer. Start liquid feeding when the fruits begin to swell. Repot each year until the tree reaches the desired size
harvesting   Pick the apples as they become ready. To test, place the fruit in the palm of the hand, lift and twist gently – the fruit should come away with the stalk intact

## FRUIT TREES FOR CONTAINERS

| Fruit | Rootstock | Shape/Form | Varieties |
|---|---|---|---|
| **APPLE** | | | |
| | M9 or M27 | Espalier, dwarf bush, pyramid, cordon | Bramley, Fiesta Greensleeves Jester James Grieve Spartan |
| | | Ballerina™ | Polka Waltz |
| | Dwarf | Mini-tree | Goldilocks |
| **PEAR** | | | |
| | Quince C | Fan, espalier, dwarf bush, pyramid, cordon, half-standard | Beth Conference |
| **CHERRY** | | | |
| | Colt or GM9 | Fan, pyramid, dwarf bush | Morello (acid) Stella (sweet) |
| **PLUM** | | | |
| | Pixy or St Julien A | Dwarf bush, cordon, fan | Victoria Marjorie's Seedling |
| **PEACH, NECTARINE** | | | |
| | St Julien A or Dwarf | Dwarf bush, fan, mini tree | |
| **FIG** | | | |
| | Pot-grown | Large bush, fan, half-standard | Brown Turkey White Marseilles |

# appendix

## *1*

### RECOMMENDED
### FRUIT AND
### VEGETABLES FOR
### CONTAINERS

**OTHER VEGETABLES AND
SALAD CROPS FOR
CONTAINER GROWING**

Aubergine
Broad Bean
Cucumber
Lettuce
Garlic
Rocket
Runner Bean
Spring Onion

## TOMATO
### *(Lycopersicon lycopersicum)*

One of the most popular plants for container growing, the tomato is easy to care for and produces a bountiful crop in late summer. The best forms for a limited space are the compact bush tomatoes like 'Red Alert' or 'Sleaford Abundance', although the taller-growing 'Alicante' and 'Outdoor Girl' can be grown if there's enough room for them to be tied in to tall canes or strings. For small cherry fruits, try 'Gardener's Delight'. There is also a variety called 'Tumbler' which is specifically designed for growing in hanging baskets.

| | |
|---|---|
| height | Bush: 30-60cm (1-2ft) |
| | Tall: 1-2m (3-6ft) |
| spread | 30cm (12in) |
| planting | Sow seed indoors on a sunny windowsill in early spring or buy small plants in late spring. Transplant into larger pots or growing bags when they reach 15cm (6in) tall |
| care | Start applying a liquid (tomato) feed when the fruits have set. Water frequently, particularly as |

the fruits are developing. When four flower clusters have set fruit (or when the plant has reached the top of the canes), pinch out the growing tip. Pinch out side shoots of taller-growing varieties as they appear between leaf joints. This will direct all the energy of the plant into producing fruit

harvesting — Pick the fruit when it is full-sized and red, but still firm. Trusses that still have green fruit at the end of the season can be brought indoors to ripen. Plants should be discarded after harvesting – seed can be collected and sown again next spring

## DWARF (FRENCH) BEANS
### *(Phaseolus vulgaris)*

Smaller than the familiar runner beans (which can also be grown in containers), dwarf or French beans are grown for their slim pods which ripen in late summer. Dwarf bush or climbing types are available; certain varieties also yield seeds which are either eaten ripe (haricot beans) or unripe (flageolet beans). For stringless, pencil-podded beans try 'Tendergreen', which is a dwarf bush, or the purple variety 'Purple Podded'.

| | |
|---|---|
| height | Dwarf: 30cm (12in) |
| | Climbing: 1.5m (5ft) |
| spread | 20cm (8in) |
| planting | Plant seeds in pots on a sunny windowsill indoors in mid-spring, or outdoors in early summer. Place the seed 5cm (2in) deep: one per 10cm (4in) pot |
| care | Keep well watered and apply a liquid feed during the growing season. Tie in the stems to bamboo canes |
| harvesting | Pick the beans when they are young and tender. Discard the plants after harvesting and sow fresh seed next year |

## COURGETTE
### *(Curcubita pepo)*

Bush varieties of the marrow plant produce smaller fruits which are harvested young and eaten as courgettes. The best variety for container growing is 'Zucchini'. The plant produces yellow trumpet-shaped flowers in summer before the fruits appear.

| | |
|---|---|
| height | 60cm (24in) |
| spread | to 1m (3ft) |
| planting | Sow two seeds per pot, 2.5cm (1in) deep in mid-spring; as the seedlings develop, remove the weaker of the two. Alternatively, buy young plants in late spring or early summer |
| care | Water frequently and start liquid feeding when the fruits begin to swell. Bush plants do not need supporting with canes |
| harvesting | Cut the courgettes when they are 10-13cm (4-5in) long. Regular harvesting will encourage the plant to continue producing fruit |

## PEPPER
### *(Capsicum annuum)*

Sweet peppers are easy to grow in containers and growing bags, where they will produce a good crop of oblong or rounded fruits in late summer and early autumn. The hardiest varieties for outdoor growing are 'Canapé' and 'Gypsy'; 'New Ace' F₁ is hardy in some areas; others can be grown if they are raised on an indoor windowsill until the temperature outdoors has risen sufficiently. There are also several decorative dwarf forms which are suitable for windowboxes and small pots: 'Fips' reaches only 18cm (7in) tall, 'Holiday Cheer' 25cm (10in). All containers should be placed in a sheltered, sunny position such as against a warm wall.

| | |
|---|---|
| height | 30-45cm (12-18in) |
| spread | 25cm (10in) |
| planting | Sow two or three seeds in the centre of a small pot in mid-spring. In cold areas, keep the pots on an indoor windowsill until early summer. Thin out the seedlings to leave just one plant, which can be left to grow on or transplanted into a growing bag |
| care | Keep well watered and begin to use a liquid feed when the fruits start to swell. Tie the stems of larger plants to bamboo canes to keep them upright |
| harvesting | Pick the fruits when they are fully grown, but still green; alternatively, leave them on the plant where they will eventually turn yellow or red. Discard plants after harvesting and sow fresh seed the following year |

## RADISH
### *(Raphanus sativus)*

An excellent salad crop for containers, radishes are grown for their edible roots, which are ready for harvesting either in late summer or in winter, depending on the variety. Summer radishes are small and round or cylindrical, whereas winter radishes tend to be large in a variety of shapes. The best varieties for summer are 'French Breakfast', which produces oval roots tipped with white, 'Long White Icicle', which is about 7.5cm (3in) long and of tapering shape, or 'Cherry Belle', which is a perfect scarlet globe with crisp white flesh. The most popular winter radish is 'Black Spanish Round' which is very hardy and has white flesh. Sowing radish seeds outdoors can begin in early spring and by sowing every two weeks or so, it is possible to have a constant supply throughout the year. In very cold areas seeds can be started indoors on a sunny windowsill in late winter. Winter sowing begins in late summer and the radishes should be ready to eat in autumn. Radishes take approximately 4-6 weeks to reach harvesting stage.

| | |
|---|---|
| foliage height | 15–30cm (6–12in) |
| foliage spread | 15cm (6in) |
| planting | *Summer varieties:* sow seeds 1cm (½in) deep in pots at least 20cm (8in) deep and 15cm (6in) in diameter. Sow in moist compost in early spring and at 2-3 weekly intervals until early summer. Thin out the seedlings if overcrowded to leave one strong plant to each pot. *Winter varieties:* sow seeds 2cm (¾in) deep in pots at least 30cm (12in) deep and 20cm (8in) in diameter. Sow in mid- to late summer in moist compost in a cool position. Thin out to leave one plant to each pot |
| care | Keep the pots well watered after sowing, particularly those sown in early summer onwards. Remove any competing weed seedlings. No feeding is necessary, but sow each batch of radishes in fresh compost |
| harvesting | *Summer varieties:* pull roots while still young – about 4-6 weeks after sowing. *Winter varieties:* pull up as required or lift the remaining crop in late autumn and store in boxes of sand in a cool, well-ventilated place until needed |

# appendix
## *2*

*RECOMMENDED*
*PLANTS FOR*
*CONTAINER*
*GROWING*

Where a particular species or named variety is given, this is more suitable for container growing than other species or varieties within the same plant group

## ANNUALS AND BIENNIALS – Spring

**Daisy *(Bellis perennis* 'Monstrosa'*)*** Miniature varieties available (B)

**Forget-me-not *(Myosotis sylvatica)*** (B) Shades of blue, according to variety

**Pansy *(Viola × wittrockiana)*** *Huge range of single and 'face' colours*

**Polyanthus *(Primula vulgaris* hybrids)** Mixed and single colours

**Wallflower *(Cheiranthus cheiri)*** especially dwarf strain 'Tom Thumb Mixed' (B)

## ANNUALS AND BIENNIALS – Summer

**Ageratum *(Ageratum boustonianum)*** (HHA)

**Alyssum *(Lobularia maritima)*** Carpeting plants in shades of pink and purple

**Begonia (*Begonia semperflorens* is a dwarf species with masses of small flowers), *B. × tuberhybrida* 'Pendula'**

**Busy Lizzie *(Impatiens walleriana)*** *Grow from seed or plug plants*

**Candytuft *(Iberis umbellata)*** *Evergreen foliage and pure white flowers*

**French Marigold *(Tagetes patula)*** (HHA) Lemon and orange varieties

**Helichrysum *(Helichrysum bracteatum)*** (HHA) Dwarf forms available

**Heliotrope *(Heliotropium × hybridum)*** *Compact bedding plant*

**Lobelia *(Lobelia erinus)*** Bushy or trailing forms available

**Petunia *(Petunia × hybrida)* Multiflora** (small-flowered) and **Grandiflora** (large-flowered) varieties available

**Mesembryanthemum *(Mesembryanthemum criniflorium)*** (HHA)

**Nasturtium *(Tropaeolum majus)*** Especially 'Alaska' with variegated foliage

**Phlox *(Phlox drummondii)*** (HHA) Dwarf forms available

**Pot Marigold *(Calendula officinalis)*** Colours range from creamy-yellow to bright orange

**Salvia *(Salvia farinacea)*** Purple-blue flower spikes

**Snapdragon *(Antirrhinum majus)*** Tall, intermediate and dwarf forms available

**Sweet Pea *(Lathyrus odoratus)*** Dwarf forms also available

**Sweet William *(Dianthus barbatus)*** (B) For cottage-garden displays

**Tobacco Plant *(Nicotiana affinis)*** Tall and dwarf forms available

## PELARGONIUMS (Geraniums)

**Ivy-leaved *(Pelargonium peltatum)*** – trailing, ivy-shaped leaves

**Regal *(Pelargonium × domesticum)*** showy flowers are usually blotched or veined

**Scented *(Pelargonium tomentosum)*** leaves have a strong peppermint aroma. Lemon, pine, orange and rose-scented pelargoniums are also available

**Zonal *(Pelargonium × hortorum)*** – bushy, leaves marked with darker 'zone'

*Primrose*

*Nasturtium*

## PERENNIALS

**Achillea (Achillea** × **'Kellereii', A.** × **'King Edward', A. tomentosa)**

**Agapanthus (Agapanthus campanulatus** and **Headbourne** hybrids)

**Aubrieta (Aubrieta deltoidea)** Spring flowering

**Bear's Breeches (Acanthus mollis)** Stately flower spikes; purple and white

**Campanula (Campanula carpatica, C. persicifolia 'Planiflora')**

**Catmint (Nepeta** × **faasenii)** Pale blue flowers with grey, aromatic foliage

**Cordyline (Cordyline terminalis)** Architectural form

**Coreopsis (Coreopsis grandiflora)** Long-lasting, sunny yellow flowers

**Day Lily (Hemerocallis fulva** and hybrids) Miniature hybrids available

**Geranium (Geranium endressii, G. pratense)** Colours include white, pink and blue

**Geum (Geum chiloense** 'Coppertone', 'Georgenberg')

**Hellebore (Helleborus niger, H. orientalis, H. lividus corsicus)** Winter and early spring flowers

**Heuchera (Heuchera sanguinea** hybrids) Red, pink or white flowers

**Hosta (Hosta fortunei, H. lancifolia, H. sieboldiana, H. crispula)**

**Michaelmas Daisy (Aster novi-belgii)** Dwarf varieties available

**New Zealand flax (Phormium tenax)** Sword-like leaves

**Oriental Poppy (Papaver orientalis)** Flowers have black blotch at base of petals

**Periwinkle (Vinca minor, V. major)** *V. major* has larger flowers and leaves

**Sedum (Sedum** × **'Autumn Joy', S. spectabile)** Attracts butterflies in late summer/autumn

## BULBS, CORMS AND TUBERS – Spring

**Anemone (Anemone blanda, 'De Caen'** or **'St Brigid')** De Caen and St Brigid are good cut flowers

**Bluebell (Scilla non-scripta)** also **S. sibirica** and **S. hispanica**

**Chionodoxa (Chionodoxa gigantea)** Also known as Glory-of-the-Snow

**Crown Imperial (Fritillaria imperialis)** Tall flowers in yellow, orange or red

**Grape Hyacinth (Muscari armeniacum, M. botryoides)**

**Hyacinth (Hyacinthus orientalis)** – for indoor forcing or outdoor growing

**Narcissus (Narcissus bulbocodium, N. jonquilla, N. cylamineus, N. poeticus, N. tazetta** and varieties)

**Tulip (Tulipa fosteriana, T. greigii, T. kaufmanniana, T. tarda,** single early and double early varieties)

## BULBS, CORMS AND TUBERS – Summer

**Begonia (Begonia** × **tuberhybrida)** Double flowered tuber – not winter hardy

**Iris** (bulbous hybrids: Dutch (early), Spanish (mid-season) and English (late))

**Lily (Lilium bulbiferum** var. **croceum, L. candidum, L. japonicum, L. martagon, L. pyrenaicum, L. regale, L. tigrinum;** Asiatic and Aurelian hybrids)

**Summer Hyacinth (Galtonia candicans)** White, bell-shaped flowers

*Lily*

*Poppy*

## BULBS, CORMS AND TUBERS – Autumn

**Colchicum (Colchicum autumnale)**
**Crocus (Crocus kotschyanus, C. speciosus)**
**Cyclamen (Cyclamen hederifolium)**
**Nerine (Nerine bowdenii)**
**Sternbergia (Sterbergia lutea)**

## BULBS, CORMS AND TUBERS – Winter

**Crocus (Crocus chrysanthus, C. imperati, C. biflorus)**
**Cyclamen (Cyclamen coum)**
**Iris (Iris histrioides major** and **I. reticulata)**
**Snowdrop (Galanthus nivalis)**

# appendix

## 2

*RECOMMENDED*
*PLANTS FOR*
*CONTAINER*
*GROWING*

**ANNUAL CLIMBERS**

Canary Creeper *(Tropaeolum peregrinum)*
Cup-and-Saucer plant *(Cobaea scandens)*

## CLIMBERS

**Actinidia** *(Actinidia kolomikta)*

**Ceanothus** *(Ceanothus × burkwoodii)* (E)

**Clematis** *(Clematis montana, C. armandii* (E), *C.orientalis, C.macropetala, C. viticella* and hybrids)

**Honeysuckle** *(Lonicera periclymenum, L. fragrantissima, L. standishii)*

**Ivy** *(Hedera helix, H. canariensis)* (E)

**Jasmine** *(Jasminum officinale, J. nudiflorum)*

**Passion Flower** *(Passiflora caerulea)* (E)

**Virginia Creeper** *(Parthenocissus quinquefolia, P. tricuspidata)*

## HERBS

**Basil** *(Ocimum basilicum)* Not winter hardy

**Bay** *(Laurus nobilis)* May be trained as a standard

**Borage** *(Borago officinalis)* Very attractive to bees

**Chervil** *(Anthriscus cerefolium)* Feather leaves used for flavour

**Chives** *(Allium schoenoprasum)* Garlic chives also available

**Fennel** *(Foeniculum vulgare)* Foliage and seeds used in cooking

**Marjoram** *(Oreganum majorana:* sweet marjoram; *O. vulgare:* common marjoram; *O.onites:* pot marjoram)

**Mint** *(Menta spicata:* common mint; *M. rotundifolia:* apple mint)

**Parsley** *(Petroselinum crispum)* Varieties include 'Moss Curled' and 'Green Velvet'

**Rosemary** *(Rosmarinus officinalis)* Blue flowers and aromatic leaves

**Sage** *(Salvia officinalis)* Purple and tri-coloured forms available

**Tarragon** *(Artemisia dracunculus)* Bushy plant with aromatic leaves

**Thyme** *(Thymus vulgaris:* common thyme; *T. × citriodorus:* lemon thyme)

## VEGETABLES

**Aubergine, Broad Bean, Courgette, Cucumber, French Bean, Garlic, Lettuce, Radish, Runner Bean, Spring Onion, Sweet Pepper, Tomato**

## FRUIT

**Apple, Blackcurrant, Cherry, Fig, Gooseberry, Grape, Nectarine, Peach, Pear, Plum, Redcurrant, Strawberry, Whitecurrant**

## SHRUBS – Deciduous

**Buddleia** *(Buddleia davidii)* Very attractive to butterflies

**Caryopteris** *(Caryopteris × clandonensis)*

## SHRUBS – Deciduous

**Daphne** *(Daphne mezereum, D. cneorum)*

**Fuchsia** *(Fuchsia magellanica* (hardy) and all tender hybrids)

**Hydrangea** *(Hydrangea macrophylla)* Mop head and lace-cap forms

**Lilac** *(Syringa microphylla)* Lilac, blue and pink varieties

**Magnolia** *(Magnolia stellata)* Star-shaped, white flowers

**Maple** *(Acer palmatum)* Especially '**Dissectum**' and '**Atropurpureum**'

**Mock Orange** *(Philadelphus microphyllus)* Strong, orange-blossom fragrance

**Weigela** *(Weigela florida)* Especially '**Variegata**'

**Winter Sweet** *(Chimonanthus praecox)*

## SHRUBS – Evergreen

**Box** *(Buxus sempervirens* '**Pyramidalis**' for clipping; '**Suffruticosa**' is a dwarf variety)

**Camellia** *(Camellia japonica)* Glossy leaves and white, pink or red blooms

**Euonymus** *(Euonymus japonicus* '**Microphyllus**')

**Heather** (Winter flowering: *Erica carnea*; summer flowering: *Calluna vulgaris*)

**Hebe** *(Hebe* × *andersonii, H.* '**Autumn Glory**', *H.* '**Bowles Hybrid**', *H. buchananii* '**Minor**', *H.* '**Carl Teschner**', *H. pinguifolia* '**Pagei**')

**Lonicera** *(Lonicera nitida* '**Baggesen's Gold**') Gold-leaved shrub

**Mahonia** *(Mahonia aquifolium)* Also known as '**Oregon Grape**'

**Mexican Orange Blossom** *(Choisya ternata)* Aromatic leaves

**Pieris** *(Pieris formosa* var. *forrestii, P.* '**Wakehurst**') Young leaves are bright red

**Privet** *(Ligustrum japonicum)* For clipping and topiary

**Rhododendron** (Evergreen and deciduous hybrids, including azaleas)

**Skimmia** *(Skimmia japonica, S. reevesiana)* Bright red berries

**Spotted Larel** *(Aucuba japonica* '**Maculata**')

## CONIFERS

*Chamaecyparis lawsoniana* **'Ellwoods Pillar'**

*Chamaecyparis pisifera* **'Boulevard'**

*Chamaecyparis pisifera* **'Nana'**

*Juniperus communis* **'Compressa'**

*Juniperus squamata* **'Blue Star'**

*Juniperus virginia* **'Sky Rocket'**

*Picea glauca* **'Albertiania conica'**

*Pinus mugo* **'Gnome'**

*Pinus mugo* **'Humpy'**

*Pinus mugo* **'Ophir'**

*Thuja occidentalis* **'Caespitosa'**

*Thuja occidentalis* **'Rheingold'**

*Thuja occidentalis* **'Smaragd'**

# PLANTS FOR SPECIAL PURPOSES

## CONTAINER PLANTS FOR WILDLIFE

**Berberis** *(Berberis buxifolius* '**Nana**', *B. b.* '**Corallina Compacta**')

**Cotoneaster** *(Cotoneaster congestus, C. conspicuous* '**Decorus**', *C. horizontalis)*

**Crab Apple** *(Malus* '**Red Jade**')

**Hebe** *(Hebe* '**Autumn Glory**', *H.* '**Carl Teschner**')

**Holly** *(Ilex aquifolium)*

**Pyracantha** *(Pyracantha angustifolia, P. atlantoides)*

# appendix

## 2

*RECOMMENDED*

*PLANTS FOR*

*CONTAINER*

*GROWING*

**ORNAMENTAL TREES**

Beech *(Fagus sylvatica* 'Purpurea pendula')
Birch *(Betula pendula* 'Youngii')
Cherry *(Prunus subhirtella* 'Pendula' or 'Cheal's Weeping')
Cotoneaster *(Cotoneaster ×  hybridus* 'Pendulus')
Holly *(Ilex aquifolium* 'Pendula')
Willow *(Salix caprea* 'Pendula')

**ORIENTAL STYLE**

Acer *(Acer palmatum* 'Dissectum')
Bamboo *(Arundinaria viridistriata)*
Flowering Cherry *(Prunus subhirtella* 'Pendula')
Corkscrew Hazel *(Corylus avellina* 'Contorta')
Fan Palm *(Trachycarpus fortunei)*
Fatsia *(Fatsia japonica)*
New Zealand Flax *(Phormium tenax)*
Yucca *(Yucca gloriosa)*

## PLANTS FOR SPECIAL PURPOSES

### DROUGHT-TOLERANT PLANTS

**Agave** *(Agave americana, A. filifera, A. parviflora, A. victoriae-reginae)*

**Artemisia** *(Artemisia abrotanum, A. schmidtiana* 'Nana')

**Curry Plant** *(Helichrysum angustifolium)* Aromatic foliage

**Hibiscus** *(Hibiscus syriacus)* Winter hardy

**Jerusalem Sage** *(Phlomis fruticosa)* Shrubby evergreen bush

**Lavender** *(Lavandula angustifolia, L. stoechas)* Strongly aromatic leaves

**Oleander** *(Nerium oleander)* Not winter hardy.

**Potentilla** *(Potentilla fruticosa* 'Red Ace', *P.f.* 'Farreri')

**Rock Rose** *(Cistus × lusitanicus, C. ladanifer;* also *Helianthemum nummularium)*

**Santolina** *(Santolina chamaecyparissus)* Silver, woolly leaves

**Senecio** *(Senecio maritimus)* Hardy in warmer regions

**Yucca** *(Yucca filamentosa)*

### ALPINES

**Arabis** *(Arabis ferdinandi-coburgii)*

**Campanula** *(Campanula arvatica)*

**Gentian** *(Gentiana acaulis, G. saxosa, G. verna* 'Angulosa')

**Geranium dalmaticum** 'Album'

**Helianthemum** *(Helianthemum alpestre)*

**Phlox** *(Phlox subulata, P.douglasii)*

**Pink** *(Dianthus alpinus, D. deltoides, D. neglectus)*

**Primula** *(Primula auricula, P. farinosa, P. marginata)*

**Saxifrage** *(Saxifraga oppositifolia* 'Splendens', *S. cochlearis* 'Minor', *S. paniculata* 'Lutea')

**Sea Heath** *(Frankenia thymifolia)*

**Sedum** *(Sedum acre, S. album, S. reflexum)*

**Thrift** *(Armeria caespitosa* 'Bevan's Variety')

**Thyme** *(Thymus praecox, T. serpyllum* 'Coccineus')

### INDOOR/OUTDOOR

*The following plants are not fully hardy and should be brought into a cool conservatory or sheltered porch during the winter.*

**Citrus** *(Citrus sinensis:* orange; *C. limon:* lemon; *C. reticulata:* mandarin)

**Bougainvillea** *(Bougainvillea glabra)*

**Fatsia** *(Fatsia japonica)*

**Jasmine** *(Jasminum polyanthum)*

**Myrtle** *(Myrtus communis)*

**Oleander** *(Nerium oleander)*

# appendix 3

**EMPTY PAINT CANS** – give them a coat of gloss to cover up the trade marks and drill holes in the bottom for drainage

**OLD CAR TYRES** – stack two or three together and fill the interior with potting compost. Choose a permanent position, because this container cannot easily be dismantled

**BROKEN WHEELBARROW** – wooden ones should be given a coat of preservative, metal ones rubbed down and painted with non-rust paint. Stand a group of small pots in the barrow and allow the plants to trail over the sides

**DISCARDED CERAMIC SINK** – cover the plug hole with a piece of fine wire mesh to prevent the compost being washed through

it. Add a good layer of drainage material such as broken crocks or clay pebbles and fill with compost

**PLASTIC BABY BATH** – drill holes for drainage and use for trailing plants which will disguise the outside. Alternatively, if you don't mind the look of it, use as a mini-pond and fill with aquatic plants

**POTS AND PANS** – kitchen utensils that have seen better days can be recycled as plant containers. Rub over with wire wool to remove any rust and place ordinary plastic plant pots of the same or slightly smaller depth inside them. Metal saucepans, enamel casserole dishes and deep roasting tins are particularly useful.

**COPPER COAL BUCKETS** – these used to stand by every fireplace and hearth but are now more likely to be found in antique shops. If you find one, clean the outer surface with proprietary copper cleaner and scrub out the inside with hot water. Choose a large plastic flower-pot to fit easily inside. Remove the inner pot before watering to prevent water collecting at the bottom of the bucket.

**CHIPPED CHINA BOWLS** – china bowls really come into their own for bulb planting. As they have no drainage holes, always use a proprietary bulb fibre which will not go stagnant when watered. Indoor china may not be frost-proof, but if the bowls are not valuable or already chipped, it is worth risking them outside.

## UNUSUAL IDEAS FOR PLANT CONTAINERS

**A quick look around the shed or garage can yield some surprising ideas for containers.**

# *USEFUL ADDRESSES*

## TREES AND SHRUBS

Highfield Nurseries
Whitminster
Gloucester
GL2 7PL

Mail order conifers, trees, shrubs, roses, fruit trees and soft fruit.

Hillier Nurseries
Ampfield House
Ampfield
Romsey
Hampshire
SO51 9PA

Hillier Garden Centres in Hampshire, Surrey, Sussex, Berkshire and Avon stock a complete range of trees, shrubs, roses etc.

## BULBS

Bloms Bulbs
Walter Blom & Son Ltd
Coombelands Nurseries,
Milton Ernest
Bedfordshire
MK44 1RQ

Mail order spring and summer bulbs, plus tender patio/conservatory plants.

Jacques Amand
The Nurseries
Clamp Hill
Stanmore,
Middlesex
HA7 3JS

Mail order spring and summer bulbs, including lilies.

## HARDY PERENNIALS

Bressingham Gardens
Bressingham
Diss
Norfolk
IP22 2AB

Mail order and plant centre; hardy perennials, shrubs, climbers, alpines and conifers.

Kelways Nurseries
Langport
Somerset
TA10 9EZ

Hostas, ferns, alpines, lilies, fuchsias.

Burncoose & South Down Nurseries
Gwennap
Redruth
Cornwall
TR16 6BJ

Perennials, ferns, lilies, rhododendrons.

## ANNUAL, BIENNIAL AND PERENNIAL SEEDS

D.T. Brown & Co
Station Road
Poulton-le Fylde
Lancs
FY6 7HX

Mail order seeds and plantlets.

# USEFUL ADDRESSES

Sutton Seeds
Hele Road
Torquay
Devon TQ2 7QJ

Mail order seed catalogue; also summer flowers as seedlings, plantlets and ready-to-pot plants.

Thompson and Morgan
London Road
Ipswich
Suffolk IP2 0BA

Mail order seed catalogue.

## ROSES

Peter Beales Roses
London Road
Attleborough
Norfolk
NR17 1AY

Mail order catalogue, including miniature and patio roses.

David Austin Roses
Bowling Green Lane
Albrighton
Wolverhampton
WV7 3HB

Mail order catalogue, including miniature and patio roses.

## GERANIUMS (PELARGONIUMS)

The Vernon Nursery
Cuddington Way
Cheam
Sutton
Surrey
SM2 7JB

Mail order catalogue. Huge range of pelargoniums, plus fuchsias.

## CONTAINERS

Whichford Pottery
Whichford
Shipston-on-Stour
Warwickshire
CV36 5PG

Guaranteed frost-proof terracotta pots by mail order or in person.

## FERNS

Fibrex Nurseries
Honeybourne Road
Pebworth
Stratford-upon Avon
CV37 8XT

Hardy fern and ivy catalogue available.

# FURTHER READING

*Hardy Ferns* Michael Jefferson-Brown (Ward Lock 1992) – a complete guide to growing outdoor ferns, including those in containers.

*The Productive Small Garden* Sue Phillips (Pelham Books 1989) – how to grow fruit and vegetables in a confined space.

*Encyclopedia of Garden Plants and Flowers* (Reader's Digest 1987) – complete 'bible' of plant species and varieties; reliable information on height, spread and cultivation.

*Wisley Handbooks Royal Horticultural Society* (Cassell) – authoritative and affordable booklets on individual plant groups, eg *Roses* by Michael Gibson and *Camellias* by David Trehane. Other titles include *Lilies, Growing Dwarf Bulbs* and *Pelargoniums*. Includes information on growing in pots.

# ACKNOWLEDGEMENTS

My special thanks to Val Burton, Ros Fischel, Richard Hanson, Mandy Little, Anne de Verteuil, Jo Weeks and Sarah Widdicombe.

Photographs by Clive Nichols unless otherwise indicated

p2 Designer: Sue Berger
p3 Coates Manor, Sussex
p6 Designer: Antony Noel
pp10–11
pp18–19 Designer: C. Cordy
pp28–9 Designer: Antony Noel
pp40–1 Keukenhof Gardens, Netherlands
pp48–9 Evening Standard Garden, Chelsea Flower Show 1993 Designer: Dan Pearson
pp58–9 photograph: Graham Strong
pp70–1 Little Bowden, Berkshire
pp80–1 The Old School House, Castle Hedingham, Essex
pp90–1 photograph: Harry Smith Collection
pp100–101 Lower House Farm, Gwent
pp110–111 Garden: David Hicks
pp118–19 Designer: Antony Noel

# INDEX

Numbers in **bold** indicate main entry

*Acanthus mollis*, 135
*Acer palmatum*, **105**, 137, 138
*Achillea*, 135
Acid-loving plants, 20, 25
*Actinidia kolomikta*, 136
African lily, 42, **84**
*Agapanthus*, 42, **84**, 135
*Agave*, 138
*Ageratum*, 134
*Allium schoenoprasum*, 136
Alpine crocus, 22
Alpine primulas, **39**
Alpines, 20, 138
    trough gardens, 24–7, 103
*Alyssum*, 134
*Anemone blanda*, **32**, 66, 135
Annuals, 31, 43
*Anthriscus cerefolium*, 136
*Antirrhinum*, **78–9**, 134
Apple, **131**
*Arabis*, 138
*Armeria*, 26, 138
*Artemisia*, 138
    *A. dracunculus*, 134
*Arundinaria*, 138
*Aster novi-belgii*, **104**, 135
*Aubretia*, **38**, 67, 135
*Aucuba japonica*, 108, 137
Autumn crocus, 23, 66

Balcony gardens, 16–17
Bamboo, 138
Bare-rooted plants, 120
Basil, 136
Bay, 108, **114**, 136
Bear's breeches, 135
Beech, 138
*Begonia*, 103, 134, 135
Bellflower see *Campanula*
*Bellis*, 66, 134
*Berberis*, 137
*Bergenia*, **38**, 108
*Betula*, 138
Biennials
    planting out, 103
    potting on, 60
    sowing, 50
Birch, 138
Birds, 60, 68
Bluebell, **53**, 135
Borage, 136
*Borago officinalis*, 136
*Bougainvillea*, 138
Box, 67, 72, 108, **114**, 137
*Buddleia*, 31, 136
Bulbs
    indoor, 92–3, 113
    lifting and storing, 50
    miniature, 26, 92
    ordering, 72
    planting, 42, 72, 92, 103
Busy Lizzie, 134
*Buxus sempervirens*, 67, 72, 108, **114**, 137

*Calendula*, 134

*Calluna vulgaris*, **84**, 137
*Camellia*, **32**, 83, 108, 137
*Campanula*, 67, **74**, 135, 138
Canary creeper, 30, 136
Candytuft, 134
*Capsicum annuum*, **133**
*Caryopteris*, 31, 136
Catmint, 67, 135
*Ceanothus*, 136
*Chamaecyparis* (dwarf forms)
    *C. lawsoniana*, 10, **14**, 77, 137
    *C. obtusa*, 67
    *C. pisifera*, 25, 108, 137
*Cheiranthus*, 66, 108, 134
Cherry, ornamental, 138
Chervil, 136
Chimney pots, 96–7
*Chimonanthus praecox*, 137
*Chionodoxa*, **38**, 108, 135
Chives, 136
*Choisya ternata*, 48, **52**, 108, 137
Christmas rose, 108, **122–3**
*Cistus*, 138
*Citrus*, 138
*Clematis*, 16, 136
    spring flowering, **44**, 60–1
    summer flowering, 21, 44
Climbers
    annual, 30
    layering, 72
    planting, 93
    pruning, 112
    supporting, 30–1
Climbing hydrangea, 16
*Cobea scandens*, 30, **99**, 136
*Colchicum*, 70, 100, **104**, 135
Compost, 20, 25, 55
    bins, 103
Conifers, 93
Containers
    choosing, 12
    cleaning and preparing, 20
    materials, 12
    mobile, 83
    unusual, 139
*Cordyline terminalis*, 135
*Coreopsis grandiflora*, 135
Corkscrew hazel, 18, **23**, 138
*Corylus avellana*, 18, **23**, 138
*Cotoneaster*, **98**, 137, 138
Courgette, **132–3**
Crab apple, 137
*Crocus*, **23**, 66, 77, 108, 135
Crocus, alpine 22
Crown imperial, **45**, 135
Cup and saucer vine, 30, **99**, 136
*Curcubita pepo*, **132–3**
Curry plant, 138
Cutting back, 21, 102
Cuttings, 31, 51, 73, 102
*Cyclamen*, 72, 100, **105**, 135

Daffodils see *Narcissus*
Daisy, 66, 134
*Daphne*, 18, **22–3**, 137
Day lily, **75**, 135
Dead-heading, 60, 73, 125
*Dianthus*, 27, 138

*D. barbatus*, 134
Dividing
    lilies, 117
    perennials, 30, 102
    snowdrops, 21
Drumstick primulas, **39**, 88
Dwarf (French) beans, **132**

*Erica carnea*, 31, 67, 108, 137
*Escallonia*, **85**
*Euonymus japonicus*, 108, 137
Evergreens
    planting, 93
    pruning, 31

*Fagus sylvatica*, 138
Fan palm, 138
*Fatsia japonica*, 138
Feeding, 43, 56, 107
    ferns, 35
    fruit and vegetables, 128
    roses, 60, 125
Fennel, 136
Ferns, 31, **34–7**, 42
Fertilisers see Feeding
*Ficus carica*, **130**
Fig, **130**
*Foeniculum vulgare*, 136
Forcing bulbs, 92–3
Forget-me-not, 134
*Fragaria* x *ananassa*, **130**
*Frankenia thymifolia*, 26, 138
French marigold, 66, **79**, 134
*Fritillaria imperialis*, **45**, 135
Frost, 113
Fruit, 128–31
Fruit trees, 128–31
    ordering, 83
    planting, 120
    pruning, 72, 121
    repotting, 21
*Fuchsia*, **63**, 92, 137
    cutting back, 21
    growing, 51
    pruning, 31
    standard, 51

*Galanthus*, **15**, 108, 135
    dividing, 21
*Galtonia*, 42, 135
*Gaultheria procumbens*, 106, 108
*Gentiana*, 26, 138
*Geranium*, 26, 135 see also Pelargoniums
*Geum*, 135
Glory of the Snow, **38**, 108, 135
Grape, **130**
Grape hyacinth, **44**, 66, 135
Growbags, 20, 128

Half-hardy annuals, 31
Hanging baskets, 54–7, 106
Hardening off, 42
Hardwood cuttings, 102
Hardy annuals, 43
Heather, **84**, 137
    winter, 31, 67, 108, 137

*Hebe*, 67, **94–5**, 137
*Hedera helix*, 67, 88, 108, 112, **123**, 136
*Helianthemum*, 26, **52**, 138
*Helichrysum*, 134, 138
Heliotrope, 134
*Helleborus*, 108, 135
    *H. niger*, 108, **122–3**, 118, 135
*Hemerocallis*, **75**, 135
Herb pots, 76–7
Herbs, 77, 88, 136
*Heuchera sanguinea*, 135
*Hibiscus syriacus*, 138
Holly, 108, **122**, 137, 138
Honeysuckle, winter, **15**, 112, 136 see also *Lonicera nitida*
Hormone rooting powders, 73
*Hosta*, **78**, 135
Houseplants, 61
Hyacinth, **32**, 66, 108, 135
    summer, 42, 135
*Hydrangea*, 31, **74–5**, 137
    climbing, 16

*Iberis umbellata*, 134
*Ilex*, 108, **122**, 137, 138
*Impatiens*, 134
*Iris*
    *I. histroides*, **14**, 26, 108, 135
    *I. pumila*, 26
    *I. reticulata*, 18, **22**, 26, 66, 88, 106, 108, 135
Ivy, 67, 88, 108, 112, **123**, 136

Japanese maple, **105**, 137, 138
Jasmine, 136, 138
    summer, 70, 73, **74**
Jerusalem sage, 138
Juniper, 25, 67, 108, **115**, 137

*Lathyrus odoratus*, 60, 134
*Laurus nobilis*, 108, **114**, 136
Lavender, 67, **84–5**, 138
    pruning, 31
Lawson cypress, 10, **14**, 77, 137

Layering, 72
Lenten rose, 108
*Ligustrum japonicum*, 137
Lilac, **62**, 137
Lilies, 42, **116–17**, 135
    see also Day lily
*Lillium regale*, 42
*Lobelia*, **52–3**, 67, 134
*Lobularia maritima*, 134
*Lonicera fragrantissima*, **15**, 112, 136
    *L. nitida*, 82, 137
*Lycopersicon lycopersicum*, **132**

*Magnolia stellata*, 28, 40, **45**, 137
*Mahonia*, **22**, 108, 137
*Malus domestica*, **131**
    *M. 'Red Jade'*, 137
Maple, Japanese, **105**, 137, 138
Marjoram, 136
*Mentha*, 77, 136
*Mesembryanthemum*, 134

Mexican orange blossom, 48, **52**, 108, 137
Michaelmas daisy, **104**, 135
Micro-drip irrigation systems, 61, 83
Mint, 77, 136
Mock orange, **62–3**, 137
Monoculture, 55
Mulching, 30, 35, 42, 125
*Muscari*, **44**, 66, 135
*Myosotis*, 134
Myrtle, 138
*Myrtus communis*, 138

*Narcissus*, 28, **33**, 66, 88, 108, 135
Nasturtium, 66, **79**, 134
*Nepata*, 67, 135
*Nerine*, 135
*Nerium oleander*, 138
New Zealand flax, 106, 108, 135, 138
*Nicotiana*, 86, 134

*Ocimum basilicum*, 136
Oleander, 138
*Oreganum*, 136
Oregon grape, **22**
Organic pest control, 68–9
Oriental poppy, 135

Pansies, 67, 88, 134
   winter, 108, **115**
*Papaver orientalis*, 135
Parsley, 103, 136
Parsley pots *see* herb pots
*Parthenocissus*, 112, 136
*Passiflora*, **62**, 136
Passion flower, **62**, 136
Patios, 121
Pelargoniums, 'geranium', 21, 134
   cuttings, 31
   growing, 50–1
   scented, 51, 86
Pepper, **133**
Perennials
   dividing, 30, 102
   planting, 93, 103
   sowing, 50
   staking, 60

Periwinkle, 67, 106, 108, 135
Pests, 68–9, 92
*Petroselinum crispum*, 136
*Petunia*, 134
*Phaseolus vulgaris*, **132**
*Philadelphus microphyllus*, **62–3**, 137
*Phlomis fruticosa*, 138
*Phlox*
   alpine, 26, 27, 138
   annual, 134
*Phormium tenax*, 106, 108, 135, 138
*Picea glauca*, 137
*Pieris*, 108, 137
Pinks, 27, 138
*Pinus mugo*, 108, 137
Polyanthus, **39**, 108, 134
Pools *see* Water gardens
*Potentilla*, 138
Pot marigold, 134
Potting on, 60
Potting-up, 31, 42
   lilies, 116
Primrose, **39**
*Primula*, 27, **39**, 88, 108, 134, 138
Privet, 137
Propagation *see also* Seeds
   cuttings, 31, 51, 73, 102
   dividing, 21, 30, 102
   layering, 72
   lilies, 117
Pruning
   *clematis*, 21, 60–1
   climbers, 112
   ferns, 35
   fruit trees, 72, 121
   roses, 112–13, 125
   shrubs, 31
   wisteria, 72
*Prunus*, 138
*Pyracantha*, 137

Radish, **133**
*Raphanus sativus*, **133**
Repotting, 21, 35, 42
*Rhododendron*, **45**, 137
Rock rose, **52**, 138
Rosemary, 136
Roses, **124–7**
   feeding, 60

ordering, 83
planting, 103, 120
pruning, 112–13
*Rosmarinus officinalis*, 136

Sage, 136
*Salix caprea*, 18, 138
*Salvia*, **85**, 134
   *S. officinalis*, 136
*Santolina*, 31, 138
*Saxifraga*, 27, 138
Scented plants, 51, 86
*Scilla non-scripta*, **53**, 135
*Sedum*, **94**, 108, 135, 138
Seeds
   collecting, 82
   ordering, 12
   sowing, 31, 43, 50, 61
Semi-ripe cuttings, 83
*Senecio maritimus*, 138
Shade, 16
Shrubs
   cuttings, 73, 102
   ordering, 83
   planting, 103
   pruning, 31
Sinks *see* Troughs
*Skimmia*, **122**, 137
Snapdragon, **78–9**, 134
Snowdrop, **15**, 108, 135
   dividing, 21
Spotted laurel, 108, 137
Spring bedding, 50
*Sternbergia*, 26, **95**, 135
Stonecrop *see* Sedum
Strawberries, **130**
Strawberry pots, 76–7
Summer hyacinth, 42, 135
Summer jasmine, 70, 73, **74**
Supports, 30–1, 60, 120
Sweet bay *see* Bay
Sweet pea, 60, 134
Sweet William, 134
*Syringa microphylla*, **62**, 137

*Tagetes patula*, 66, **79**, 134
Tarragon, 136
Tender plants, 92
Thrift, 138
*Thuja occidentalis*, 25, 108, 137
Thyme, 136

*Thymus*, 27, 86, 108, 136, 138
Tobacco plant, 134
Tomato, **132**
Tools, 121
Trees *see also* Fruit trees, Conifers
   bare-rooted, 120
   ordering, 83
   ornamental, 138
   planting, 103
   trimming, 112
*Tropaeolum majus*, 66, **79**, 134
*Tropaeolum peregrinum*, 30, 136
Troughs
   alpine gardens, 24–7
   ferns, 34–5
Tulips, **44–5**, 92, 103, 108, 135

Vegetables, 128, 132–3
*Viburnum tinus*, **14**, 108
*Vinca*, 67, 106, 108, 135
*Viola x wittrockiana*, 67, 88, 134
   'Universal' (winter), 108, **115**
Virginia creeper, 112, 136
*Vitus vinifera*, **130**

Wallflower, 66, 108, 134
Wall pots, 86–9
Water butts, 61
Water gardens, 46–7, 113
Watering, 21, 43, 56, 61, 82–3, 107
   ferns, 35
   roses, 125
Water plants, 47
Weeding, 35, 72
*Weigela florida*, 48, **53**, 137
Wildlife plants, 137
Willow, 18, 138
Windowboxes, 64–7, 106
Winter displays, 77, 106–9
Winter heather, 31, 67, 108, 137
Winter honeysuckle, **15**, 112, 136
Winter pansies, 108, **115**
Wintersweet, 137
Wisteria, 72, 112

*Yucca*, 106, 108, 138